Emotional Mechanics

STOPPING PI(E)

YOCHANAN STOPPI

Emotional Mechanics: Stopping Pi(e)

ISBN 978-0-578-72915-2

Table of Contents

Table of Contents

DEDICATION

This book is dedicated to my wife, who supports me and encourages me in everything that I do. Without her and her support, I never would have been able to undertake this project. My life has vastly improved since we have met, and I would give the world to her if I could.

This book is dedicated to my father, my grandfather, and the Stoppi family tree. For only through pain does wisdom blossom, and this family has seen its share of tragedy and pain. As the Stoppis fell, they still maintained a fleeting smile. As Neil Young said: We were right, we were giving, that's how we kept what we gave away.

This book is dedicated to all of those who suffer from mental illness, those who have committed suicide, those who suffer from addiction, ones haunted by the memories of premature deaths, and best friends and family who have stopped talking to each other. May Saint Dymphna help provide you solace along with this book.

FOREWORD

I am inspired. Seriously.

As a family psychologist, I have observed, studied, taught, and counseled a variety of individuals, from children to adults, who were struggling with a variety of mental health, addiction, and adjustment issues. Thus, I am no stranger to the nuances and complexities of mental illness.

I have also read many books, self-help guides, memoirs, articles, and workbooks on a vast array of mental health conditions, such as general anxiety disorder, social anxiety, PTSD, OCD, clinical depression, bipolar disorder, and schizophrenia.

Although the material was informative, there has only been one book that has managed to awaken me in ways I never imagined. That book is "Emotional Mechanics" by Yochanan Stoppi.

For the first time in a really long time, I am inspired to re-examine my life, and more specifically, my choices to see where I can make the necessary changes to experience the best life possible – for me. This book has made me question my truth. At times

I agreed with his revelations and at other times, I questioned them, but regardless they made me think.

I do not struggle with mental illness; however, Stoppi inspired me to forgive myself and others, so I can achieve a continuous state of comfort, peace, tranquility, and serenity.

He has made me want to "get to know myself better." His words have made me ponder what I really believe and why. He has stirred something deep inside simply through his use of mathematical formulas and patterns and poignant narratives and examples.

What makes "Emotional Mechanics" so thought-provoking and life-changing is the journey Stoppi takes us on. He shares the most vulnerable parts of his life with us in a way that lingers in the mind and heart several chapters later. He is honest and raw.

Stoppi has struggled throughout his life. He has lost loved ones, friends, opportunities, and romantic interests due to his illness, fear of losing himself, and alcohol abuse.

Yet, you root for him and rightfully so, because he is a fighter.

He lays it all out to provide real relief (tips and suggestions) to those still struggling with mental health issues. He doesn't try to make you think or feel a certain way. He simply presents the information in a way that reaches a logical reader with the same intensity and relatability as an emotional one. Examples and personal narratives are used to strengthen the text, while footnotes and formulas are used as points-of-reference, guides, and/or emotional anchors.

Stoppi has managed to combine compassion and a spirit of hope in his book – a belief that one's destiny lies in his own hands through the choices he makes. This is the sentiment I often stress to individuals who feel helpless and hopeless. It's all about choices and a will to change.

"Emotional Mechanics" is a revolutionary new understanding of how bipolar, anxiety, addiction, and suicide are interrelated. It helps readers understand that they have the tools needed to attain the life they have always envisioned.

It is a powerful page-turner that validates that no one is beyond hope. No trauma, chronic illness, addiction, rejection, or heartache is "irredeemable."

We all make mistakes. It's what makes us "human." Stoppi is no exception. But, what really matters is what we do when we fall down. Do we continue on the path we are on or do we make the necessary changes for a more positive future outcome?

Stoppi believes that a mentally ill person can experience "freedom" and I agree. However, acquiring this "freedom" takes courage, determination, and a strong belief that you have the power to choose your own path.

It is for this reason that I'll be recommending this riveting book for many years to come. This book can and will change how you think about yourself, others, and the world around you. It will challenge you. You just have to keep an open heart and mind.

Listen. Think. Absorb. Act.

Sincerely,
Dr. R. Y. Langham
Psychologist

PREFACE

This book was developed through the experiences of painful life events—such as, mental illness, alcohol abuse, divorce, bankruptcy, poverty, abandonment, and poor health. These events plagued my mind continuously until I could explain why they hurt me so much. This book was also developed by observing others going through similar situations, and how my reflections and advice helped them negotiate these painful emotions.

INTRODUCTION

The purpose of this book is to lend some of the insight I have gained through living through painful events to others so that they may benefit from what I have learned. This book dissects much of what is considered fluid or intangible into more solid forms that may be grasped or manipulated.

Most of the information in this book is presented from personal experience, personal reasoning and analysis, and original ideas. There are a few citations, but the reader is encouraged to evaluate what he or she considers useful or true, and to read the rest as an exercise in thinking. I think everything I stated within the book is truthful, although it is impossible to prove this.

The anecdotes, examples, and analysis presented herein is given to illustrate concepts, thoughts, or feelings. They are not necessarily reflective of my personal beliefs or absolute truths. It is the belief of this author that nothing is completely true that nothing is completely false. The comparisons made between the sexes are not always true, they were made for illustrative purposes, and I am not prejudiced with regards to sex, race, religion, or any other feature. However, I am willing to compare and collate the myriad of differences that exist within these features in an effort to understand people and life. The world has become too insular with regards to these differences, and, indeed, it has isolated humanity.

In Chapter 1, the book begins with showing how society at large is responsible, in part, for people's negative feelings, habits, and attitudes towards life. Chapter 2 prescribes definitions for all of the emotions and feelings that are discussed and analyzed throughout the book. It is not necessary to read Chapter 2 in its entirety; the reader may consult it for specific definitions for certain emotions and feelings as they reach those specific chapters in the rest of the book. The appendix contains tangents and extrapolations of certain ideas that were developed in the book.

CHAPTER 1: IT'S NOT REALLY YOUR FAULT

The title of this chapter either resonates with you or sounds like a cop-out. People often refuse to take ownership of their faults or shortcomings, and often blame them on other people or some type of societal system, like an employer. However, you wouldn't be reading this book if you thought everything was right with the world. And I wouldn't be right for putting everything on you. A big part of everyone's problems is society at large. The evidence is in the numbers: one out of every seven people has a diagnosable mental illness. The DSM IV has 297 disorders listed. The number of therapy and counseling services is at an all-time high. Each person has a 50 percent chance of experiencing at least one major mental illness event in their lifetime[1]. These statistics apply to the US, but I would imagine they're similar in other developed countries. They are different in third world countries, where depression is actually less prevalent. This is from one of

1 https://www.cdc.gov/mentalhealth/learn/index.htm

my favorite YouTube videos, and is actually an analysis of a scene from the movie *Blade Runner*, but summarizes what I'm trying to get at here:

> When a system becomes an individual and we individuals realize that we have become the system—following orders with a sense of fleeting rigidity
>
> The system asks us to stop for a moment and evaluate ourselves to see what we have become: a dehumanized society shaped by capitalistic and technological excess.
>
> We're attached to our memories, the feelings from these memories and the sense of purpose derived from these memories. The desire to exist in a world filled with cruelty and unfairness. It's a question of empathy, which seems to be disappearing from the world.[2]

CAPITALISTIC AND TECHNOLOGICAL EXCESS

We live in a dehumanized society shaped by capitalistic and technological excess. Judging by our society alone, some alien or outsider would conclude that the purpose of our lives was to invent new things that served no other purpose than to make people buy them, for these new things to be fueled by technology, and for this technology to enable us to exist in increasing degrees of isolation from and disillusionment with people and the real world. This has been going on for a long time, but over the past twenty years cell phones, the internet, and other sophisticated communications technology have really enabled this state. We are inundated by a constant pressure to buy new things and

2 https://www.youtube.com/watch?v=GbXIONSjmkY

upgrade things that already work just fine. We really don't need a new cell phone every year. Do people really need to be able to control their home's heating, lighting, and security with a cell phone from anywhere in the world? I feel like the inventions have become increasingly pointless, and companies are running out of things to make us buy. I have watched eleven seasons of the popular show "Shark Tank," where entrepreneurs pitch new companies, inventions, and business ideas to billionaire investors. Most of the new creations on the show are new foods, personalized subscription services that are soldvia the internet (like new razors for shaving), gimmicks for pets, or new toys for children. Basically, people are inventing things they think will sell.

In an earlier age, inventers created things that were designed to make people's lives easier. The washing machine, for example, ended up saving women hundreds of hours of labor a year. Those hours could be used for other things. So let's say those extra hours were put into cooking. Everyone in the family got to experience better meals because of the washing machine. Still, Mom had just replaced one chore with another. Some years later, the microwave was invented. This enabled the household cook to prepare meals more quickly whenever they decided to forego use of the oven. With this extra time, something else could be done—like say, cleaning up after dinner instead of getting Junior to do it. Then, the dishwasher was invented, and it allowed Mom to clean up faster. Without the extra chore, Junior could spend more time on his homework and maybe watch some TV before bedtime. The point here is that every invention, every time saver, every convenience is just used to make room for more work, more technology, or more leisure. Leisure is normally last on the list.

The interesting thing about these inventions is that they were initially designed to last and function well. A Maytag washer purchased in the 1950s, with some maintenance here and there, could easily last thirty years. How do I know this? When I was young, my family was poor so we couldn't afford a new washing machine. We had someone's old Maytag that was thirty years old. It worked fine. These lasting devices were bad for business, and now washing machines last for about seven years, despite seventy years of technological progress. How do I know this? Every washing machine I purchased as an adult has lasted for five to seven years. The part that had to be replaced in order to fix it cost almost as much as a new machine. Now every time a washing machine breaks, it doesn't get fixed. It gets replaced. Relationships have also become this way. Once they're damaged, people just write each other off. They don't try to repair the relationship. The new part that's required to fix the relationship costs more than the relationship is worth. The new part is a part of yourself that you're unwilling to give or are unwilling to change.

The societal focus became getting people to be consumers and to buy things. High profits, corporate greed, boredom, and laziness all contributed to this. The first two are from society. The latter two—boredom and laziness—are us. People shop because they have nothing better to do or because of the high[3] they get from it. We literally bought into it. But, really, we were sold by it, before we bought into it. Very cleverly, it was sold, and we purchased our way into our own slavery.

After we all became consumers, the technology really started to change our society in inescapable ways that we are still adjusting to. Technology was supposed to connect the world, but it separated it. Technology was supposed to make us more capable, but it just burdened us. Technology was supposed to make our

---

3 You can bet your bottom dollar that shopping releases dopamine the same way cocaine does.

lives easier, but it just made them more hectic. Technology was supposed to make communication easier, but the tried and true, thousands-of-years-old *conversation*, has eroded and is now an endangered species.

IT'S NOT SOCIETY'S FAULT EITHER

In the beginning, society and inventors didn't know what they were doing when they were inventing this stuff. I mean, they had short-sighted goals of improving lives or improving profits. They did not really consider the long-term implications of their inventions. All they were concerned with was "Can I do it?" and not "Should I do it?" Did the inventor of the cell phone ever picture a family out to eat, with each family member's face buried in his or her phone, with all of them completely out of touch with each other? That would have been hard to imagine back then. Did anyone ever expect to be broken up with via a text message? Did anyone ever think their entire school would see nude pictures of them? Of course not. But it's not entirely the inventor's fault. It's still people who *choose* to use technology this way.

IT'S A QUESTION OF EMPATHY, WHICH SEEMS TO BE DISAPPEARING FROM THE WORLD.

Consumerism and technology create personalized experiences and marketing that make people feel like they're the only ones who exist. Who wouldn't buy something if they felt like an item or service was crafted specifically for them? With targeted and smart advertising, this is sort of true. Marketing and products are placed very carefully before us, and we buy them—we buy them like never before. Most of these new products are technologically oriented, but they don't have to be to make people love technology or things more than they love people. People become things, and if the people aren't marketed towards them like a product is, they show little interest or empathy. In a strange amalgam of events, most of our interactions with strangers are while making purchases in an old-school brick-and-mortar shopping experience. I recall walking through a shopping mall when an attractive woman approached me, eagerness in her eyes and a shimmer of hope, trying to sell me something. When I said no, her eyes instantly went blank and she walked away. Her mark was gone and she was seeking another one. What bothered me was how quickly her eyes seemed genuine and how quickly that expression faded into oblivion. The transition in her eyes was exactly the way someone looks at you before they recognize you, and then do—but in reverse. I became a stranger stranger to a stranger. Fifty years ago, there would have been more conversation in the parting; maybe she would have said, "Okay, well have a nice day." Or, maybe I would have said, "I just bought one but thank you for offering." We didn't. We were each a steak to each other. You don't empathize with steak or think of where it comes from. You either eat it or you send it back to the kitchen.

The two biggest drivers of lack of empathy are lack of face-to-face communication and the lack of hearing people's voices. When the telephone was invented, it took away the face. When the cell phone and internet were invented, they took away the voice. We are met with poorly written emails and text messages and emoticons rather than the warmth or force of a face-to-face conversation. The inflection of voices is gone. An entire region of the brain, the fusiform gyrus[4], could have gone dormant. It is

---

4 This part of the brain specifically evolved to recognize, analyze, and interpret faces. It is only present in human beings, even though dogs also have the ability to interpret people's faces. Dogs are the only animals on the planet that can do this.

said that 90 percent of communication is nonverbal. This means that, at best, we are getting 10 percent. With emoticons, maybe we get 12 percent ;) In old science fiction films, the video call is often shown as a popular high tech invention. That technology has been widely available for some time, but it withdraws us from our digital curtain, and text messaging is used instead. I have never seen a single science fiction movie that showcased text messaging as some revolutionary technology. Thirty years ago, if you saw text messaging in a movie, would you be impressed by it? No. "That's a stupid invention," you would say. My most charming usage of video chat was back when instant messaging was popular on the internet. After IMing for some time with a girl, we would decide to video chat. I remember the thrill of getting to see her face for the first time. Anyway, in youth's defense, I notice that children use FaceTime more than the telephone. Meanwhile most adults use the regular phone, except when they call their children. Facetime should be renamed FamiliarFaceTime. What's better than seeing a familiar face?

I think it is necessary to see people's faces, shake hands, and hear people's voices—at the very least—to feel their humanity. I think it's necessary to feel someone's humanity in order to empathize with them. I think it's necessary to empathize with someone to feel sympathy and compassion for them. I think compassion is necessary to truly love someone. Empathy is the catalyst for sympathy, sympathy for compassion, and compassion for love. This chain reaction is expressed as:

Face to Face Interaction→Humanity
Recognition→Empathy→Sympathy→Compassion→Love

The ultimate expression of love and compassion is total self-sacrifice in an act of compassion *for someone who hates you.*

Such people have been described and venerated in religions, and rightfully so, even if you don't believe they existed or even if they didn't exist. The idea of self-sacrifice for someone you don't know or who hates you is one of the most powerful ideas in the universe. I have composed a poem that describes this:

> **Love created life so that life could experience love.**
> **Life, so experienced, might love life enough that it**
> **would give life for the sake of love.**

IT'S THE SENSE OF TOUCH

This is dialogue from the movie *Crash* (2004):

> **Graham Waters:** It's the sense of touch.
>
> **Ria:** What?
>
> **Graham Waters:** In the real city you... you walk. You know? You brush past people. People bump into you. In L.A. nobody touches you. We're always behind this metal and glass. I think we miss that touch so much that we crash into each other just so we can feel something.

This dialogue plays out in the opening scene of the movie where the characters, two detectives, are investigating a car accident. The movie takes place in Los Angeles. Apparently L.A. is unlike New York, where it's so crowded that a city walker has to brush past people to move around. City comparisons aside, there are many people who go extended periods of time without touching someone or being touched. And when I say touch someone, I mean touch at all, even a simple handshake.

For a period after my divorce, I lived the single life in a city very close to Manhattan. In fact, I worked in Manhattan. Between work during the day, solitary dining, solitary walks, and Netflix at night in my apartment alone, I didn't touch anyone. I didn't touch anyone for a long time, until I eventually started dating someone. In my world, I would get the occasional business handshake, but that was it. Compared to my later life, which was filled with hugs and kisses from children, goodnight kisses, profuse hugs, and a very touchy and lovey spouse, I was really deprived. I wouldn't admit it back then, but I missed being touched.

Another "fun" thing I noticed was how late in the day it could be before I first spoke to someone. This can go on longer than you'd think. If you live alone, you already have guaranteed silence until you leave the apartment. You're catching the train, but there's no way you're going to talk to anyone there, unless someone asks for information about the train schedule or you do. Then it's the final walk into the office. You may say hi to someone on your way in, but you may not. You can get to your desk still not having said a word that day. Then the countdown begins: when will someone call on the phone or come into your office to ask you something? Prolong that by putting on headphones. You may get to lunchtime without having said a word to any human soul. Congratulations.

Before the insular technological age, people spent their free time engaging in various social outlets: clubs, dance halls, community centers, organized sports, recreational sports, bars, clubs, the Boy Scouts, or whatever else was prevalent back then that has since faded. For example, I became a Master Freemason, and the Lodge[5] told me, as I was being initiated, how there was much less interest

5 In Freemasonry, the Lodge is both the physical building the members meet in and the term that refers to the collective membership of a particular Lodge, which serves a certain geographical area.

in the fraternity than in years past. In fact, the Lodge had watered down their initiation requirements because people did not have the spare time necessary to remember the recitations that are necessary for full admission. Those past social circles had plenty of rounds of back slaps, hugs, touching dancing, and other human contact that we all miss out on now. For the working family man or young professional, life centers around work and some of its social extensions (like a company mixer before an optional training seminar). The young professional will complete their social life with a romantic partner or, perhaps, the bar or club scene. The working man or woman with a family has their second role as the family man or woman. A stay-at-home parent is isolated, but has some social contact with other parents during extracurricular events, parent-teacher conferences, and things like that. This doesn't describe all the modern variants, but it describes many. None of them have enough social interaction to satisfy the basic human need for that interaction. This results in loneliness, and the love of goods, gadgets, and technology. I have to say, when I'm feeling a certain way, and I can call upon literally thousands of songs to console me, it helps, albeit temporarily. The gadgets and the ability to extend an enhanced digital version of ourselves feels good.

POINTLESS POWER

I can reach into my pocket at any time and pull out a device that has more computing power than all the computers that were used in the Apollo moon missions combined, summon a large portion of humanity's collective knowledge in a second, listen to any song I can think of, perform complicated computations via voice dictation, call anyone in the world, video chat with anyone in the world, buy anything I want, send money to anyone I want, collect money from anyone I want, watch any show or movie I want, find a person to date, determine my exact position on the earth including my elevation, measure the length of a sidewalk, check out the pitch of a staircase, measure how level something is, take five thousand pictures, take videos with various effects, edit photos and videos, record sounds, and download an application, ad hoc, for a specific purpose that hitherto wasn't contemplated. And, of course, this device can do millions of things that I am not listing, and thousands of things I don't know it could be used for. This device is the modern smart phone. It's millions of devices in one. If someone from a hundred years ago saw all the things a person could do and know with such a device, they would think the person was a god. But guess what? If you take away the meaning that's necessary to want to do all those things and appreciate the things that device can do, it's powerless.

The world must pique your curiosity before you want to explore it. The people have to be meaningful to you in order for you to want to contact them. You have to be excited at the prospect of dating before you sign up for an online dating service. The world has to be experienced firsthand, physically, and viscerally, for the digital world to mean anything. The physical world has to mean something first. What we have now is the digital world supplanting the physical one. Or, the digital one being learned in parallel with the real world. Or, the digital world being learned before the physical one. I feel lucky that I am the last generation that grew up without the internet. This puts me behind a line so thick and so substantial that even 56,000[6] bits could easily fit along its width.

---

6 A 56K modem, transmitting at 56,000 bits per second, was the last dial up modem used in "dial-up" internet connections.

REVERSE THE EROSION

Even if we are only willing to admit to some of the societal factors that have led to isolation, loneliness, and mental illness, they are there, and they are hurting almost everyone. What do we do about it? The answer is simple. Go back to doing what we used to do and what our parents did. We can't, because things are so different? That's true. We can't go all the way back; however, we can reverse the priority of things and people, and that would change everything again.

Don't bring cell phones to the dinner table. Actually talk to each other. Listen. It's very difficult to listen nowadays. It's harder than it's ever been. Attention spans are shorter than ever, and people love technology more than they love people. Technology tends to treat people better than other people do, so this is understandable. But listen and see what happens. Push yourself to do it. Nothing makes a person feel better than being listened to when they speak. What comes after listening? Respond to what they said or ask a question if you want them to clarify something or speak more about something. Hopefully they will do the same thing to you. What's this? This is a conversation!

Don't go to the bar to talk to people. It just results in drunk talk, drinking buddies, and bad habits. Find some social club to join. It could be a sports club, a fraternity, or even a support group. Even if you don't really need a support group, you can go there to help others and it's a good way to socialize.

Ask someone to join you in an activity you enjoy. It can be a trip to the gym, a round of golf, or a walk in the woods. It doesn't matter what it is. The important thing is doing it together with someone and talking to them. Don't put headphones on to listen to music while you're with the other person. The other person is your music and you're their music. One time, my son asked me to come to his room to watch him play video games. I said okay. When I got to his room, he had his headset on and was talking to his online friends. I laughed and walked out.

Get a card for someone. Tell them you appreciate them. Say something sappy. Say something romantic. Surprise them. Some people are so emotionally deprived that a simple thing like this will melt or break their heart, and they will cry in response to your simple kind gesture. I don't cry as much as I should, but receiving a simple "I Love You Daddy" from my children, with some detail included in it that I didn't know they noticed, has moved me to tears on more than occasion.

MACHINE MEN WITH MACHINE MINDS AND MACHINE HEARTS!

I will end this chapter with a speech. This speech may be the best speech of all time.[7] It's from the movie *The Great Dictator*, which was directed by and starred Charlie Chaplin, the great comedic actor of the twentieth century.

> I'm sorry, but I don't want to be an emperor. That's not my business. I don't want to rule or conquer anyone. I should like to help everyone—if possible—Jew, Gentile—black man—white. We all want to help one another. Human beings are like that. We want to live by each other's happiness—not by each other's misery. We don't want to hate and despise one another. In this world there is room for everyone. And the good earth is rich and can provide for everyone. The way of life can be free and beautiful, but we have lost the way.

---

7 The full power of the speech can only be achieved by actually listening to it. See https://www.youtube.com/watch?v=J7GY1Xg6X20 or google it to find the video or audio of it.

Greed has poisoned men's souls, has barricaded the world with hate, has goose-stepped us into misery and bloodshed. We have developed speed, but we have shut ourselves in. Machinery that gives abundance has left us in want. Our knowledge has made us cynical. Our cleverness, hard and unkind. We think too much and feel too little. More than machinery we need humanity. More than cleverness we need kindness and gentleness. Without these qualities, life will be violent and all will be lost....

The aeroplane and the radio have brought us closer together. The very nature of these inventions cries out for the goodness in men—cries out for universal brotherhood—for the unity of us all. Even now my voice is reaching millions throughout the world—millions of despairing men, women, and little children—victims of a system that makes men torture and imprison innocent people.

To those who can hear me, I say—do not despair. The misery that is now upon us is but the passing of greed—the bitterness of men who fear the way of human progress. The hate of men will pass, and dictators die, and the power they took from the people will return to the people. And so long as men die, liberty will never perish. .....

Soldiers! don't give yourselves to brutes—men who despise you—enslave you—who regiment your lives—tell you what to do—what to think and what to feel! Who drill you—diet you—treat you like cattle, use you as cannon fodder. Don't give yourselves to these unnatural men—machine men with machine minds and machine hearts! You are not machines! You are not cattle! You are men! You have the love of humanity in your hearts! You don't hate! Only the unloved hate—the unloved and the unnatural! Soldiers! Don't fight for slavery! Fight for liberty!

In the 17th Chapter of St Luke it is written: "…the Kingdom of God is within man"—not one man nor a group of men, but in all men! In you! You, the people have the power—the power to create machines. The power to create happiness! You, the people, have the power to make this life free and beautiful, to make this life a wonderful adventure.

Then—in the name of democracy—let us use that power—let us all unite. Let us fight for a new world—a decent world that will give men a chance to work—that will give youth a future and old age a security. By the promise of these things, brutes have risen to power. But they lie! They do not fulfil that promise. They never will!

Dictators free themselves but they enslave the people! Now let us fight to fulfil that promise! Let us fight to free the world—to do away with national barriers—to do away with greed, with hate and intolerance. Let us fight for a world of reason, a world where science and progress will lead to all men's happiness. Soldiers! in the name of democracy, let us all unite!

CHAPTER 2: DEFINING EMOTIONS

In everyday language, people refer to emotions all the time. "I'm so mad at my boss right now!" or "I hate my parents." We've heard it all before. The way people use language to express or relay their emotions to others has a huge impact on the emotions they feel themselves. The way people use language stems from the definitions of the words themselves. We define most of the words we know by association or by listening to the context of sentences. Emotions and feelings, as we shall see, build upon each other like branches of a tree. In order to understand this tree, the emotions, the branches, have to be defined precisely. This is exactly what this chapter intends to do, and these definitions will form the basis for how these terms are used in later chapters. People loosely use certain words to describe their emotions or their emotional state. While this conveys information that can be useful, more precise and streamlined results could be achieved in processing these emotions or experiencing their passing if they were defined and discussed precisely. What's more, the inception and tree-like branching of emotions and feelings, when understood, can also be used to achieve this effect.

This chapter need not be read in its entirety. The reader may skip to the next chapters and refer to this chapter when a specific feeling or emotion is encountered and a formal definition becomes helpful. This chapter's exact definitions of emotions and feelings are necessary to fully understand concepts that are presented later.

Emotions aren't just like trees though. They don't always grow into something larger and more complex. Sometimes, a spontaneous realization or thought can prune away branches of a feeling and reduce it to a much simpler emotion. Sometimes, the transient building and holding of a feeling can cause an explosion that results in smaller fragments of feeling that manifest in isolation separately from each other. There are variables of consciousness that grip and manipulate feelings and sculpt them into other ones. These processes sometimes take—or can at least be described by—logical operators, mathematical notation, and other variables in the same way that physical phenomenon can be described by mathematics and science. The neurochemistry, hormones, and physical processes that take place simultaneously as, before, or after emotions are experienced are exceptionally complicated and are not the subject of this book; however, I have researched these subjects and they are beyond interesting although they escape my full comprehension.

Emotional mechanics involves the willful observation of these branching and mechanical relationships, and offers the reader the chance to use conscious intervention, structured thinking, and the realization of where certain feelings and emotions come from in order to change their way of thinking, prolong or shorten the duration of feelings, understand their feelings, and ultimately improve their lives. This approach aims to stop the cycle of the chaotic nature of thinking and emotions from controlling our lives in ways we don't want.

An attempt to define the following emotions, feelings, or states of mind follows. These feelings, emotions, and mindsets are:

Anger	Anxiety
Fear	Disgust
Respect	Nervousness
Effort	Pride
Irritability	Embarrassment and Shame
Jealousy	Guilt
Envy	Regret
Greed	Trust
Comfort	Hatred
Peace	Love

ANGER

The most primitive emotions are anger and fear. We are all familiar with anger. What exactly is anger though? Why do we get angry? In my observations, I have categorized three basic reasons why people get angry. I call them the Three Laws of Anger. They are as follows:

I. A person feels angry if their ego, or self-perception, is damaged by the action or inaction of others, an event, or anything else.

II. A person feels angry when they have to perform more work than they otherwise would have performed, due to an event that occurred, a person ordering them to do it, or through some accident.

III. A person feels angry if they are physically hurt, by accident or on purpose, or upon reflection of a past injury.

These are pretty broad Laws, and I challenge you to think of situations or things that make people angry that do not fall into at least one of the three laws above. Anger, in its basic form, is a temporary inflation, or crutch, or stilt, for a person to temporarily perch on in response to a situation. This is akin to the basic fight or flight response. If a threatened animal decides to fight, anger builds them up by injecting their body with stress hormones, adrenaline, and sends blood to critical muscles in the anticipation of a fight. In real life, anger does the same thing to someone's mind and body. It's like Newton's Third Law of Motion: the reaction to the three laws is anger. The purpose of the anger is to inflate a person's size or inner stature so they can react to the real or perceived damage inflicted. Figure 1-1 shows an inflation to anger in response to a threat.

Figure 2-1: Anger Inflation

There is an expansive category of anger that falls into each of the three laws mentioned above. There are many times a person is so emotionally mixed up for so long that they are very confused about the way they feel. They can't identify individual emotions anymore. Every feeling descends over their being in a sort of haze. In some instances, prolonged feelings like this can cause gastrointestinal distress, general uneasiness, or even physical pain. When someone is frustrated, confused, or damaged by feelings they can't identify or process, they often default to anger. Again, anger is used to temporarily inflate someone as a means of self-defense. It doesn't matter if the true nature of the threat is actually unknown, or that this threat is coming from within. This is true physically and emotionally.

FEAR

Fear may be even more primal than anger, because most people experience fear more often than anger. If the opposite is the case, it is possible that anger may just be a mask for fear. Overt fear is less acceptable in our society, particularly for males. This is also a reason anger is used to mask fear. Fear is felt after an assessment of a potential threat is performed. The assessment goes like this:

THREAT>ME → Fear

THREAT < ME Anger or Comfort

If it is the first case, it will prevent more damage to yourself to flee or act reserved than it would take to use the energy to confront or endure the threat. Note that assessments of both the threat and self need to be made simultaneously, and the potential results of avoiding the threat versus not avoiding the threat also have to be simulated within the mind.

So defined further, we have the following assessment when a threat produces fear:

The threat, despite any efforts on my behalf, will cause imminent damage that will take more time or effort to recover from than the time or effort required to remain hidden from the threat or to flee from the threat.

In other words, it's worth the time and energy to run away or lie low and wait for the threat to pass. In animals, this fear is primal and instinctive. Each animal is programed via evolution to avoid certain predators. In humans, other humans are the threat. The threat situations are most often emotional, mental, or involved with some aspect of society (as opposed to a threat from the jungle). It could be the domineering boss who we are afraid will fire us if we get out of line. If we get fired, we will have to find another job before our finances become seriously compromised.

We do not have any instincts enabling us to fully recognize threats from other people. They are almost entirely concocted processes. In any event, both an assessment of a potential threat and an assessment of self take place before fear is permitted to run its course. A person with low self-esteem and confidence tends to experience fear more often—not necessarily because their threat assessment is high, but because their assessment of self is so low.

Therefore, to summarize:

Fear = Threat > Self (in the threat capacity) and when:

Projected Fear Cost < Sustained Self Damage Cost

RESPECT

The word respect has been so overused and diluted that it's begun to lose meaning. Nevertheless, we will take a splash into respect and its related feelings and emotions. Respect is related to fear. Respect is related to assessing someone's capacity or abilities as being of great magnitude. I hesitate to say "assess their abilities in a positive way," because a lot of respect is earned by people displaying their ability to create negative results—e.g., inflict damage upon someone via physical violence. Young children exhibit fear, but they are not capable of respect. It is too complicated an emotion for them. This is why children don't listen out of respect for their parents. Children listen out of fear of punishment. This is a characteristic of the child mind versus the adolescent or adult mind.

Respect is when someone assesses someone as wielding a high ability, skill, capability, or quality and simultaneously makes the judgment that that person is wielding those things in a morally acceptable, internally congruous, or somehow otherwise favorable way. If a person makes the first assessment and reaches the opposite judgment, the resulting feeling could easily, but not always, be fear. Respect is, then:

Respect = assessment of quality with great magnitude + wielding quality in an acceptable way

Often, someone fears someone before they respect them. For instance, one may meet a very large, muscular, strong man in the gym to later find out that he has a docile, benign personality. This creates respect because someone with such great strength could easily get away with acting arrogant or outwardly hostile. Figure 1-2 describes the process of fear-or-respect evaluation.

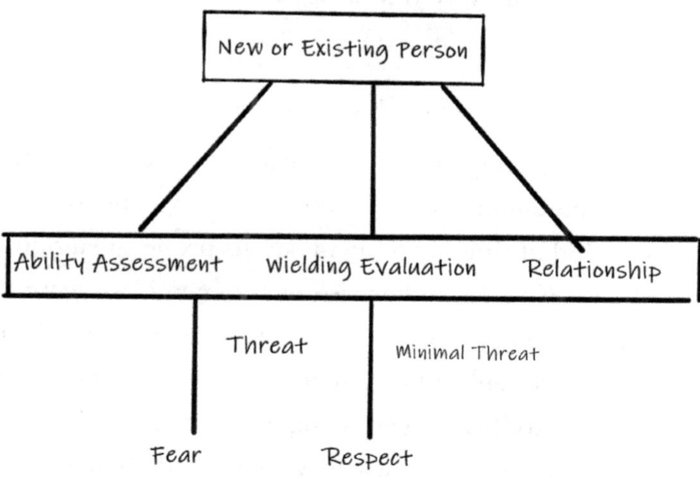

Figure 2-2: Respect vs Fear Flowchart

EFFORT

Effort, exertion, fatigue, and endurance are all related to emotions and feelings, how we express them, and how one emotion or feeling evolves into another. Let's examine effort in the mental or emotional context. We have all been told to "pay attention." When we're told to "pay" attention, what are we paying with? We're paying with effort for a sustained period of time, because it takes mental exertion to focus on one particular thing among an infinite amount of stimuli within and without. Attention isn't just a discrete act of effort—it is a sustained process of exertion. Mental exertion is the energy consumed during mental focus, thinking, or experiencing a certain feeling or emotion. Exertion is akin to the physics definition of work, which equals power times time or force times distance. When a negative feeling is experienced, it takes mental exertion to endure that condition or feeling in the same way that a person endures physical pain. Exertion is:

Exertion = Effort x Duration

Fatigue is the feeling of decreased capacity to do or feel things based on the amount of exertion experienced or applied during a particular period of time. Fatigue makes us prone to emotions or feelings that we wouldn't otherwise experience if we were fresh and filled with energy. Remembering the second law of anger (becoming angry when we have to do more work), we are particularly susceptible to this trigger of anger when we are tired. More specifically, we are irritable when we are tired. Being irritable means we are easily angered or pushed to feel negative feelings.

Endurance is simply the resistance of fatigue, and the ability to experience long bouts of mental effort or feelings without a substantial decrease in performance, energy, or changed (towards the negative) feelings from baseline. The relationship between fatigue, energy, exertion, and endurance can be described as:

Overall Fatigue Level is: (Baseline Energy – Exertion) / Endurance

Endurance is when the change of effort divided by the change in time, or, for math experts, the derivative of effort with respect to time is small enough over the entire period so as to maintain an acceptable level of performance:

This is the exact same relationship for overall fatigue level, except it is stating that there may be a time during the instant exertion level, say where the hill is too steep to climb during a bike ride, rises to a level that is temporarily insurmountable. That is to say, we can ride our bikes for the entire ten-mile bike ride, but we don't have enough power to go up the steep hill in the middle of the ride.

Which is saying:

Effort > Power

The "Δ" in this notation is simply "the change of," and is used in Calculus and other math subjects.

We often run into situations in mental health where we can endure a day, but a critical ten minutes, say, during a panic attack, are unbearable. For these unbearable situations, we have to have preplanned responses to go to in order to successfully navigate those steep hills. Here is an example of some emergency coping skills or activities one can do to endure these unbearable moments:

- Call a friend or emergency counselor
- Practice deep breathing
- Go out for a walk or start exercising
- Take a shower
- Ride a bicycle
- Go for a nature hike
- Go to the gym
- Listen to music
- Isolate yourself
- Surround yourself with people
- Take an "as needed" medication

These measures may not completely take away the unbearable feelings, but hopefully they can lessen them to a degree that you can tolerate until they abate. This book attempts to provide other tools that one can use to effectively navigate these rough waters.

IRRITABILITY

Irritability is a feeling that is strongly related to fatigue. The more fatigued we are, the more susceptible we are to the spectrum of things that irritate us. For example, sometimes at the family dinner table, my kids smack their lips as they are eating. If I was fatigued by my day, I would be more prone to getting irritated by this and would probably tell my children to stop smacking. On the other hand, if I had a good day and still had ample amounts of energy, I might just let it go and would not feel particularly irritated by it. Irritability is the condition whereby an observation causes a desire for the subject of the observation to cease or reduce some or all forms of the observation, or to lash out at the person or thing that caused the irritation. Irritability leads to action when the instantaneous ability to bear a negative feeling drops below the energy level required to endure it. This was just expressed within the Effort Section.

Certain irritants are almost universal; others are idiosyncratic. Take two different people, and one person may be irritated by a particular thing and one may not. The number of times the irritant has been experienced also plays a factor as to whether or not someone is irritated. Going back to my dinner table example: if my child repeatedly chewed with their mouth open, I would be far more likely to become irritated with them because of all of the times I nicely, or not so nicely, asked them not to do it.

Irritation is defined as thus:

P(irritation) = Past Experience with Irritant + Number of Repetitions of Irritant + Fatigue Level of Individual

P(irritation) is the probability that an event might irritate someone. It is expressed as a probability because of the uncertainty associated with it. It is interesting to note that as past experience with a new irritant increases, idiosyncratic irritants emerge, and that's why this term appears on the right hand side of the equation. The Number of Repetitions of Irritant is, of course, based on past experience, but it is more specific to a certain irritant, and that's why it's a discrete term. The fatigue level has already been discussed.

Consistent irritation results in the decreased comfort of an individual. A decrease in comfort leads to an increase in effort required to sustain oneself without change. Continuous irritation can exist because a person was asked to cease the irritating behavior and did not stop. These two conditions provoke the second and first laws of anger, respectively, and eventually result in anger.

JEALOUSY

In Star Wars, Episode III: The Revenge of the Sith, Yoda states "...jealousy, the shadow of greed that is." This is a succinct enough description of jealousy, and the exposition that follows is totally unnecessary.

Jealousy begins when one assesses that something favorable is being bestowed upon another person, deservingly or undeservingly—it doesn't matter. Or, alternatively, that something favorable has happened to another person, whether it was earned or unearned. The person performing the assessment then compares his or her own condition to this other person and gauges the difference. This difference becomes unacceptable when the other person has taken a superior vantage point in the assessing person's mind. This feeling is different from envy, which is discussed later.

Jealousy, as Yoda said, is essentially greed in disguise because the assessing person is resenting the fact that they were not bestowed with a favorable thing or condition whereas someone else was. It is not unlike a greedy person who is trying to get everything for themselves. Jealousy leads to anger because it satisfies the first law of anger (anger resulting from self esteem damage).

In the movie "Hector and the Search for Happiness," Hector makes the statement "Making comparisons can spoil your happiness." Jealousy cannot begin without a comparison, so the predecessor to jealousy is the need to compare. We can write this relationship, as well as its final terminus to anger, as:

Comparison → Assessment of Inequity → Awareness of Lower Position → Jealousy → Anger

Jealousy is a linear process. It's like a chain. As we progress from one step to the next, we move closer to getting jealous. To prevent jealousy, break any one of the links in the chain: don't compare, don't think someone is getting more than you, don't think you are lower than someone because they have something you don't, don't resent someone because you feel lower than them, and even if you get all the way to the end you can still break the chain by not getting angry if you do become jealous. Examine your jealousy, and perhaps you may be able to make it disappear before you do something out of spite or, worse yet, revenge. Jealousy is discussed in detail in Chapter 7.

ENVY

Envy is the sister emotion to jealousy, with some critical differences. Envy is merely coveting the possessions, status, achievements, or other things that another person has. It is simply the desire to have something that someone else has, and it is prompted by observing that this other person has it. The object of the envy could be something the person already wants, but it's almost like it's advertised by someone else having it. Envy is like a child wanting a toy after seeing a commercial for it on TV. Envy is discussed in Chapter 7.

GREED

Greed is the driving force behind jealousy. It is the desire for *more* no matter how much is received. It is the belief that everything that is available and desirable should come to you at the expense or pain of others. Greed is never satiated by obtaining anything. And what do you benefit if you gain the whole world but lose your own soul?[8] . Greed can only be vaporized by other means, as we will see in Chapter 7.

COMFORT

Comfort is not an emotion, but it's a feeling that is related to the favorable acceptance of one's current emotional state, physical state, and physical surroundings. It is a goal sought by many. When it is not achieved, or is disrupted, negative emotions abound. Anxiety is related to comfort. In fact, anxiety is almost the polar opposite of comfort.

---

8 Matthew 16:26

Comfort is the acceptance of one's surrounding environment, state of mind, company, ambient sounds, lighting, temperature, and other things with a desire for none of those things to change, or to change to an even more comfortable state with little to no effort. Comfort is a sign that some desire was achieved, albeit a low-key type of desire. Comfort could be walking into an air-conditioned office after being outside in the heat for a prolonged period. Comfort could be the satiation of thirst. It could be a combination of things: an easy chair by a fireplace, a glass of bourbon on a side table, a good book to read, and a quiet environment. Comfort can normally be disrupted by something that causes some form of exertion that deviates from the comfortable state. For example, I could be comfortable sitting here writing this chapter and someone could ask me to take the dog out. While I know the dog needs to go out, I am comfortable writing, and would rather continue to do so, without interruption, than take the dog out. From Animal Collective's *What Would I Graze? Sky*:

Comfort, comfort why do you run for it?
Why can't you keep doing
What you're supposed to do?
Why can't I reach you?
When I most need you
You're at the beach and
I'm in some strange bed

To try to sum it up in our familiar notation:

Comfort = Desire to maintain current state > desire to change state

In other words, in the absence of an external stimulus or task we have to perform, when we are comfortable, we are likely to remain in our current state for as long as possible.

Conversely to all of this, if comfort is sustained for some certain amount of time, inaction itself can cause an uncomfortable feeling or a feeling of restlessness. This is a result of the internal state changing to one that is incompatible with the outer state. An example of this is someone spending half of their weekend watching Netflix and eating snacks, only to suddenly have the desire to go outside and "do something." Comfort, sustained too long, can result in boredom, which results in changing one's environment or activity.

PEACE

Peace is relatively simple. In history and in literal terms, it's the absence of war. In the realm of the mind, peace is when the resolution of a certain issue, feeling, or emotion occurs. In this sense, we say, "I'm at peace with the loss of my mother. I have accepted it and moved on, although I will always remember and cherish her."

There are greater degrees of peace within the mind that can be expressed by terms such as tranquility, serenity, bliss, contentment, and even nirvana. These latter terms express lasting peace over many, if not all, tormenting thorns of the mind.

Some people get nervous when they realize they are at peace. They think of it as the calm before the storm. They know that peace is temporary. If peace is based on external factors, it certainly is temporary, because there will be events, subject to negative interpretation and emotions, that will occur.

Achieving serenity or nirvana is the goal of spiritual gurus, masters, and people with a high degree of spirituality. It is one of the highest expressions of self-actualization, although it ironically involves the denial of self.

ANXIETY

Anxiety is the most prevalent mental illness. In fact, it is so prevalent that many consider it normal, and it's not considered a mental illness at all in its less severe forms. Being the most common mental illness, it has the least social stigma. If someone confesses to someone that they have anxiety issues, the other person would typically at least empathize, and, quite possibly share that they have a similar condition.

What is anxiety? It's related to fear for sure, but it's markedly different. It differs mostly in its origin or cause, intensity, and duration. Anxiety is a general worry that something, somewhere, will or is about to go wrong. What's more, this worry concludes that, if something does go wrong, the individual himself will be harmed, his family will be harmed, his future conditions will be harmed, or something else to that effect. The consequences imagined when feeling anxiety tend to have a chain reaction effect that takes something menial and raises it to the level of catastrophic. The threshold at which the anxiety kicks in lowers the more it is experienced. For example, someone might be afraid of getting sick. When they see someone with symptoms, they try to avoid them and think nothing more of it. After a couple of years and after a few more bouts with the flu, they will see someone with flu symptoms and avoid them like they had the plague. What changed in the interim such that the threshold of anxiety was decreased? Anxiety can develop into obsessive compulsive disorder or OCD. Essentially OCD is specifically provoked anxiety that is remediated by repetitive thoughts or rituals. The remediation is only temporary, and the rituals and provoking anxiety are strong enough to prompt the sufferer to avoid certain situations or conditions that elicit the obsessive compulsive acts.

Anxiety is really a fear of the universe in general, its tendency to change, and our inability to control it. Anxiety is the belief that a perpetual state of readiness, worry, or nervousness will defend against the universe's changes. It is the tensing before the starting gun fires. While anxiety may be useful sometimes, because it does achieve its goal, it is normally groundless. People will remember the one time out of a hundred anxious feelings helped them in life, but they will forget the other ninety-nine when it was a waste of time and energy. Anxiety becomes a waste of energy, and eventually begins to break the body and mind down. Anxiety causes many people to turn to drugs, alcohol, and prescription medications for relief. We will see later some techniques and thoughts that help alleviate anxiety. For now, anxiety can be defined:

Anxiety = Fear of the universe > acceptance of the universe; therefore: costs of being on edge > benefits of being calm and at peace

This definition may seem unfair, because the second inequality involves a choice. People say that reducing their anxiety is impossible, and that they have tried everything. They may have tried pruning the branches of their anxiety, only to have them grow back faster every time, but they never reached the root of their anxiety. This is why their anxiety persists. People become more comfortable being trapped in their anxiety than taking the choice to confront it. In order to take the choice to confront and evaluate one's anxiety, it has to be determined that:

benefits of being calm and at peace > costs of being on edge

Both of the factors in this inequality are enormous. The sufferer must summon, as a magician summons the magic of nature, a supernatural level of willpower to want to benefit from being calm and at peace with their anxiety. Without this motivation, they will remain jailed by their anxiety.

Anxiety really has a probability associated with it. Or, more precisely, a risk tolerance. Risk is defined, in engineering and other fields, as:

Risk = Probability of Event x Consequence of Event

The consequence is always something negative. Essentially, anxiety is signaling that the continuous risk, which increases as time increases, because time increases the cumulative probability, is intolerable without a continuous state of uneasiness, readiness, or vigilance.

DISGUST

Disgust is accepted in many texts as being a fundamental emotion. This was surprising to me, because I never considered it an emotion at all. I considered it a reaction. Emotions are a sort of reaction, so that could be a fair assessment. Humorously, the first time I encountered disgust as a primary emotion was in the Disney movie *Inside Out.* This movie features a bunch of characters, each representing an emotion in a child's mind, swaying her to make decisions and showing her reactions to situations by virtue of these characters in her mind. In the movie, the primary emotions are Joy, Sadness, Fear, Anger, and Disgust.

Disgust is an aversion, a dislike, a recoil, a feeling of revulsion, sometimes a certain sickness to the stomach, and other avoidance responses to something. In kids, it often results in the proclamation, "That's disgusting." The same thing, to a different kid, can also result in the exclamatory, "That's so cool!" So, while the feeling of disgust is universal, the things that trigger it couldn't be more different. This is the interesting aspect of disgust that needs to be well defined and explored. We will do this in Chapter 11.

NERVOUSNESS

Nervousness is related to anxiety, as defined before, but it has a more immediate and focused reason for being. Nervousness is experienced in the waiting room of the doctor, in anticipationg of the feedback from the doctor or some uncomfortable medical procedure that is about to take place. Nervousness occurs when we know we are about to be brought out of our comfort zone. In other words, nervousness ensues when we know our level of effort is going to increase to sustain a certain situation. The situation prompting nervousness may be one that was uncomfortable before, one with a high degree of uncertainty about what is going to happen, or one that has a defined threat as discussed in the Fear section.

Nervousness prompts a heightened sense of vigilance, perception, and threat perception. It is usually justified, and fades after the prompting situation passes. Repeated exposure to the same situation without incident leads to a decrease or complete elimination of nervousness for that particular situation.

Uncertain Situation: Past Discomfort ; Defined Prior Threat →Nervousness ↑

Situation Passes; Repeated Exposure to Same Situation→Nervousness↓

PRIDE

Pride entails the feelings associated with internal reflection of past accomplishments, attained material possessions, or a positive assessment of current abilities. This self-awareness is sometimes enough to evoke a certain amount of pride. On the other hand, it may evoke no pride or even a feeling of low self-esteem. For this definition, we will assume that the subject possesses a positive feeling about what they are reflecting on. Potential pride stems from the receiving of accomplishments, recognition of character, or third-party validation. Pride can be anticipated, and the prideful person may position the manifested prideful accomplishments more prominently in order to feel prouder. On the other hand, they may not do anything to increase the chances of anyone becoming aware of the source of their pride, or may even make an effort to hide these things. In this event, pride is felt when one person becomes aware of something positive in another person and expresses or conveys approval of those things, which in turn translates into approval of that person. Sometimes, this process is spontaneous: a compliment is given about something that was not ever expected by the receiver of the compliment. The pride process described above takes place spontaneously, and pride is felt.

People are afraid to feel proud of things, lest others don't validate the prideful feelings. People are afraid to be proud, because overly proud people can easily come off as arrogant, and other people may belittle or diminish their pride by criticizing them or berating the source of their pride. A popular Bible verse reinforces this idea:

> *Pride goeth before destruction, and an haughty spirit before a fall.*
>
> *—Proverbs 16:18, KJV*

The popular saying is more succinct: "Pride goeth before a fall." This alludes to the probability of a person failing because they are prideful. Or even that failure is imminent if someone is proud of anything. How can this be? How can we feel good about ourselves if we're never proud of ourselves or if we're nervous anytime people compliment us or notice a good thing that we've done?

This verse and ideas are too negatively interpreted. What this verse *could* mean is that one must have positive or high feelings for anything beforehand in order for it to eventually be toppled over or "destroyed." It's sort of like saying that you have to climb up a hill before you can roll down. It's a simple cause and effect statement. However, it doesn't say that pride has to go before a fall. Genuine pride, expressed with tact, does not have to go before a fall. A haughty spirit will most likely incur a fall, and probably should do so.

Here are the chain links for pride increasing and decreasing, respectively:

Positive Assessment of Current Status, Achievements, or Possessions→Self or Other Awareness of These Things→Pride

Positive Assessment of Current Status, Achievements, or Possessions→< of Self or Other Awareness of These Things→Pride↓

People may be proud of something for a while, only for the feeling to fade as they become more mature or interested in other things. A twelve-year-old whose team has just won the Little League championship will certainly be proud. After twenty years, this feat will become a mere fond memory. Pride is like a sculpture. How it endures time and exposure to others is related to how and why it was constructed to begin with. Indeed, some sculptures outlast lifetimes. These pride sculptures that transcend lifetimes remain pride sculptures while people who knew that person are still living. Beyond that, a pride sculpture could become a monument to a notable person in history, who has, in some way, done something in his or her life that is important enough to be remembered.

EMBARRASSMENT AND SHAME

Embarrassment and shame are related to each other by some simple variables, and are also related to pride by other variables.

Embarrassment is a feeling set up by a condition whereby someone else suddenly, and sometimes surprisingly, becomes aware of something that is determined by either party to be potentially negative, unsavory, or illustrates a mistake on behalf of the embarrassed person. The key feature of embarrassment is that the thing to be embarrassed by is not a direct, unavoidable feature of the embarrassed person. A child who is poor may be embarrassed that he has to wear cheap clothes even before another person points it out, and even more so after someone points it out. A boy may be caught with his zipper down as someone else points this out; this causes embarrassment even though the boy had no prior knowledge of it and becomes aware only through someone else. Although embarrassment is faultless and does not involve previous intent, its victims often feel regret and bitterness about the condition that led to the embarrassment. This is an understandable, but unjustified, response. It is important to note that someone can feel embarrassment even if someone else did not express awareness of the embarrassing condition. This is called *self-consciousness,* but really it is just potential embarrassment.

Self-Consciousness = Latent Embarrassment

Possibly the biggest sources of self-consciousness are aspects of our physical appearance. For unfair reasons, our society considers taller people, both men and women, but especially men, to be superior to shorter people. This simply isn't true, but taller people are often placed in higher job positions, leadership roles, and enjoy other advantages that short people don't. What's worse, is that women strongly desire taller men. In fact, women prefer men who are 8 inches taller than them[9]. This would mean that the average woman, at 5'4", would prefer a man who is 6 feet tall. Only 16 percent of men are this tall or taller. As such, if this height requirement were etched in stone, an average-height woman would be ruling out 84 percent of all suitors. This may not sound that important, but it is of great importance, as one's ego, future, and potential spouse may be affected by something as superficial as height. Short men are usually self-conscious about their height, and are often very angry and bitter about their stature. It was hard for me to empathize with this until one of my girlfriends, standing at 5'9", which is pretty tall for a woman (97th percentile for a woman and 50th, average height, for a man), "jokingly" stated that she wished I were a bit taller, perhaps 6'4" or 6'5". I'm 6'1", which is the 91st percentile for men. Then, she said she was joking, even though she said it more than once. Then I realized that 6'5" is exactly 8 inches taller than 5'9", so I realized she was actually being truthful. 6'5" is in the 99.6th percentile in height, so that would include only 1 out of every 250 men. Of course I would want to be perfect for any girlfriend, so for the first time in my life I felt short, and a little bit of resentment over

---

9 https://www.psychologytoday.com/us/blog/after-service/201909/5-reasons-why-women-and-men-care-about-height

my height. I was more bitter towards her preference, and not at my actual height. I would rather be 6'1" than 6'5".

Shame is a feeling set up by a condition whereby someone else suddenly, and sometimes surprisingly, becomes aware of something that is determined by either party to be potentially negative, unsavory, ***and*** may illustrate a deliberate act or intention that violates morality, laws, norms, and the rules of acceptable behavior. The shamed person is normally aware of the shaming condition before it becomes exposed to someone else. This prior awareness can sometimes come with guilt, but that is not always the case. There are other times when a person feels shamed only when the shameful act is pointed out and becomes exposed. The morality level of a person is the variable that determines whether they feel guilty beforehand. Shame, like embarrassment, can also be a spontaneous process. During the course of someone suddenly pointing out a potentially shameful act, the receiver has to make an assessment as to whether they performed the act willfully and if indeed it was a negative action. In these situations, debates and arguments of this condition can erupt. The potentially shamed person can justify their act and avoid feeling shame. The observer can attempt to shame the person without the receiver feeling shamed. Shame is relative and can depend on how much context is known about the potentially shameful act.

Here are the notations of embarrassment and shame:

Embarrassment = Exposure of a Faultless Negative Condition to the Awareness of Others

Shame = Embarrassment + Acknowledgement of Ill Will or Fault

GUILT

Guilt is related to shame, but not always. Guilt is an acknowledgement that one has performed an act that was injurious to others, was immoral, destroyed the property of oneself or that of others, or some other damage combined with the recognition that there were better alternatives to these acts. There is a feeling of remorse that the act occurred, a potential desire for remediation, and an urge to alleviate the guilty feelings. Someone who is guilty may feel the need to confess. This need to confess can scale all the way up to confessing to an act of murder. In other words, the urge to confess is so strong that a person may choose to do it even if such a confession would imprison them for life. The novel *Crime and Punishment* is a perfect example of this. The protagonist murders someone and is driven mad by his guilt. He eventually confesses.

Guilt is a lingering feeling that can last a long time. A person can choose to live with their guilt, do something to "make up for it," apologize to someone, forgive someone else, or even forgive himself. What's more, guilty feelings can lead to other, somewhat unrelated decisions that are questionable. For example, a father who spends too much time at the office working may buy his children gifts instead of spending more time with them. The "making up for it" feature of guilt is potentially destructive. Making up for it can also be fruitful and consist of a simple apology. An apology whose sole purpose is to alleviate guilt is not a complete, sincere apology. We present our guilt chain:

Reflection Upon a Previous Act→Recognition of Wrongdoing→Remorse, Remediation, Alleviation = Guilt

REGRET

Regret is the desire to change, or undo, something one did, said, or chose in the past. It can arise from guilt, shame, and embarrassment. Regret leads to "What if" statements. "I regret not getting that job. What if I had gotten that job...? My life would probably be better now." Intrinsic to regret is the belief that if the regretful condition were taken away or reversed, things in the present would be better. I can't sum it up better than this:

"Regrets are a waste of time. They're the past crippling the present." —From Under the Tuscan Sun, 2003

TRUST

Trust is one of the most difficult feelings to describe, and one of the most difficult things to feel. This is ironic, considering "In God We Trust" is printed on our money. For sure, no one trusts anything about money. Our society has devolved to a state where few people trust each other. When there is no trust, the exchange between people becomes limited. There are also degrees of trust, and perhaps these degrees can be measured. A parent may trust their teenager to go out for the night and come back at a prescribed curfew, but they might not trust that same teen to take their credit card with them.

Trust is the belief that another person would act in your best interests unwaveringly without hesitation. What's more, total trust ensues when a person is comfortable bestowing power over themselves to another person without knowing precisely what the person will do with that power and responsibility. In short, total trust is acknowledging that another person or entity knows your bests interests better than you do and will act or make decisions with that in mind. This is the implicit meaning behind "In God We Trust."

The reason trust is so difficult to achieve is that most people, first and foremost, act in their own self-interest. This is done even if others are damaged in the process. For this reason, and because people default to fear, distrust, and possibly disgust when they meet someone new, trust is never achieved upon first meeting someone.

Also, negative actions carry greater weight than positive ones. This goes back to the jungle. If a hunter is walking through the bush and hears a rustling sound, they could assume it's a tiger and take cover. Or, the hunter could assume it's the wind and do nothing. If it is the tiger, the consequences could be serious injury or death. If it's nothing, there are no consequences. Each time the bush rustles and nothing happens, inaction is reinforced. When the time comes that the rustling is actually a tiger in the bush, the complacent hunters become an easy meal for the tiger due to their lack of vigilance. On the other hand, there can be a lifetime of vigilance, and the rustling of the bush never turns out to be a tiger. Finally, a period of vigilance with the wind rustling the bush is followed by an incident where the tiger appears and is avoided due to that extra vigilance. One mistake of not assuming it's the tiger can result in death.

If this example is too archaic, consider the modern age. A celebrity takes years, or even an entire lifetime to build a positive reputation. It only takes a single scandal, crime, or period of negative press to permanently ruin that reputation. In the universe, actions, from a thermodynamics standpoint,[10]

---

10 It's simply the Second Law of Thermodynamics. This basically states that entropy, a measure of disorder, is always increasing. Even if you clean your room put everything in order, the air molecules within the room that were moved around by your increased energy output were disrupted more than the order the room-cleaning effected. There are ways to measure forms of this in more basic applications.

are always irreversible. Once the toothpaste is out of the tube, it can never go back. Positive actions carry lower weight than negative ones. A single positive act, in itself, cannot change your life. A single positive act can cause a chain reaction that can extensively change your life, but it takes time and careful observation to matter. For these reasons, my father used to always say "One 'ah shit' wipes out ten 'atta boys.'" In graver situations, he would say "One 'ah shit' wipes out a million 'atta boys.'" The gravest version of this is "One 'ah shit' wipes out your entire life and the future of your children."

There are two major impediments to trust. The first one is that negative actions, or mistakes, carry more weight than positive ones. The second is that positive actions are judged to be negative ones. People don't trust that other people were doing things with their best interests at heart. A better way of saying this is that people don't trust that people were doing things in good *faith.* Trust without full understanding, belief, or conviction is actually a definition of faith. Faith is going out on a limb. Faith is necessary before trust is earned. Trust in God is an acceptable level of understanding and belief that God has your best interests in Him. Faith is when tough times are ahead or when trust has gotten derailed. In a fully trusted person, once full trust is earned, when a questionable act is observed it is met with queries of wisdom and understanding, trust is intact, and trust can be further cemented after an explanation is given. After the explanation is given, understanding increases, and the beneficiary can become wiser and better from this process. The demonstration of justifiable actions, wisdom, feelings, and love are all things that cement trust even when actions or responses are not fully understood. We conclude this section with the trust and faith relationships:

Faith = Trust – Sufficient Understanding

Faith = Trust + Adversity

Total Trust = Good Faith Actions + Wise Explanations + Time + Love

Unconditional Love = Total Trust + x + y +...

HATRED

Hatred is simply ill will towards something, someone, or a condition, that desires for it to be diminished, eradicated, or damaged. If you hate someone, you most likely will be happy if something negative befalls them. At the very least, if something negative happens to them, you won't have any sympathy towards them.

This is pretty straightforward, until we consider the fact that most people who are strongly hated have previously been loved. This famous quote confirms this:

Heaven has no rage like love to hatred turned, nor hell a fury like a woman scorned. —William Congreve

After we are rejected, we try to diminish whatever it was that we were attached to from the start. It's the toddler at daycare who gets a toy taken away from them. "I didn't like that stupid toy anyway!" This is sufficient for a rejection from something we merely liked. If the rejection was from a person who was loved, hatred can erupt, and revenge can even be sought from that person. Possessions can be destroyed, photos can be released, secrets can be exposed, and anything else that can cause harm.

If someone hates someone from the start, the rejection is the possibility that the person could have been someone they liked or loved. They are rejecting the person because they have to deal with someone they hate instead of someone they love. One has to know love in order to know hate.

LOVE

Countless songs, stories, poems, and movies have been written and played out in an effort to describe love. All of them combined may not be adequate to define it. Robert Heinlein wrote that "love is that condition in which the happiness of another person is essential to your own." That is the best, most succinct definition of love I have stumbled upon. Exactly the opposite to hate, we build up, inflate, proudly display, and reflect upon the people and things we love.

Love typically has its opposite as hate. It is easy to hate someone we used to love. Love can have an opposite; however, it is the *one thing that doesn't have to have an opposite to exist.* Hate is dependent upon knowing love lost. One cannot hate without loving first. One knows love before one knows unconditional love; unconditional love is reflexive.

The pure form of love is unconditional love. This is love of everything, and is based upon the acceptance of everything, serenity, bliss, and nirvana. This type of love radiates as awareness radiates, as the conscious mind radiates, and as the universe expands. *Figure 2-3* illustrates this. Nirvana, bliss, and serenity are the sought after points in many religions and spiritual practices. The main reason many fail to reach these points, are because these points begin within, and can't be found without. Jesus said:

> *And when he was demanded of the Pharisees, when the kingdom of God should come, he answered them and said, The kingdom of God cometh not with observation:*

Neither shall they say, Lo here! or, lo there! for, behold, the kingdom of God is within you.
—Luke 17:2

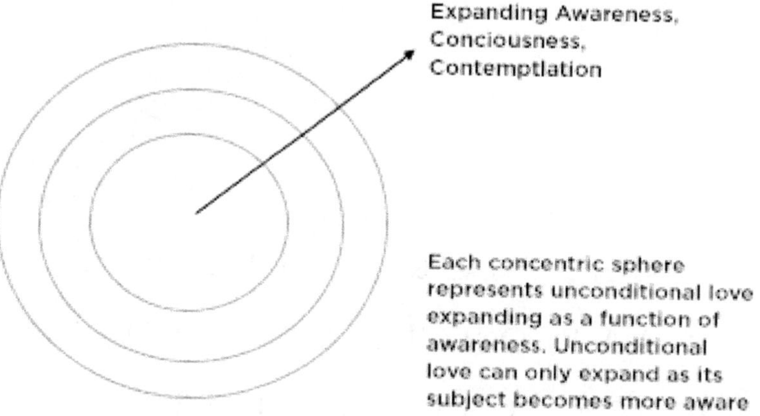

Figure 2-3: Unconditional Love has No Opposite

CHAPTER 3: THIS > THAT OR THAT > THIS OR THIS = THAT?

In the movie "The Deer Hunter," there is a part where Mike, the character played by Robert DeNiro, repeatedly says, "This is this.[11]" The other characters are confused, and they display this confusion, but what Mike meant is never clarified. I suppose the phrase "This is that" would be even more confusing, because at least the words are the same in the former version.

If we were still in Chapter 1, where there were some rants about technology, I would point out that computers, communications signaling, and electronics all operate on the basis of two signals: 1 for on and 0 for off. All the complicated operations of an iPhone, the laptop I'm writing on right now, the smart TV you may be watching, and anything else based on electrical signals communicates this way. Indeed,

11 https://www.youtube.com/watch?v=VlmanKoPLyo

any number can be expressed in "binary," as just ones and zeroes. The scary thing, especially if you believe that robots may eventually take over the world or that "The Matrix" might actually be true, is that humans think in zeroes and ones too —0, 1, and 2...okay, I'll stop.

DUALITY

Every aspect of reality and consciousness —feelings, emotions, sensations, judgments, the basis of comparisons, extent, range, color, and everything else—can be expressed or bounded by two polar opposites. What's more, you can't know one without the other. As a simple example, I can tell you that, surely, you cannot know light without knowing darkness. That's elementary, you might say. Certainly everything else can't be described like that! But it can, and actual things, this or that, lie on a spectrum of each of these polar opposites. The polar opposite pairs that are most damning, as we will see, are good or bad and right or wrong. These combinations are really just "this or that" from a certain perspective.

Love cannot be known without knowing hate. Love is the condition in which someone accepts everything someone does for the sake of love. Hate is the condition whereby someone rejects and scorns everything someone does on the basis of their hatred for them. The similarity between the two is that their purposes are reflexive. Have you ever hated someone to the extent that literally everything they did angered you? Have you ever loved someone so much that they never seemed wrong no matter what they did to you? Figure 3-1 illustrates a hate-love linear spectrum. The entries on it are for illustrative purposes only.

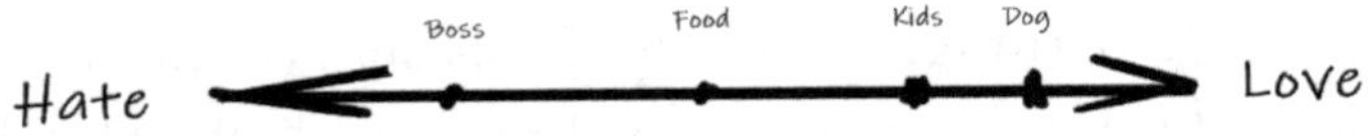

Figure 3-1: Hate Love Spectrum

A line cannot be known without knowing a curve. In baseball, this is the difference between a fastball and a curveball. A perfect line is a straight line, the shortest distance between two points. A perfect, constant curve is a circle; the curvature around a center point is constant. However, when a circle gets very large, its surface seems straight. This is the reason why for thousands of years people thought the world was flat. A circle can be completely described by the length of its diameter, a straight line, and the number Pi (that 3.14 number that goes on forever). Pi is the ratio of a circle's circumference to its diameter. This concept is integral to the title of this book. Figure 3-2 illustrates the definition of Pi, which isn't the actual number itself. The actual number of Pi itself is unknown to this day.

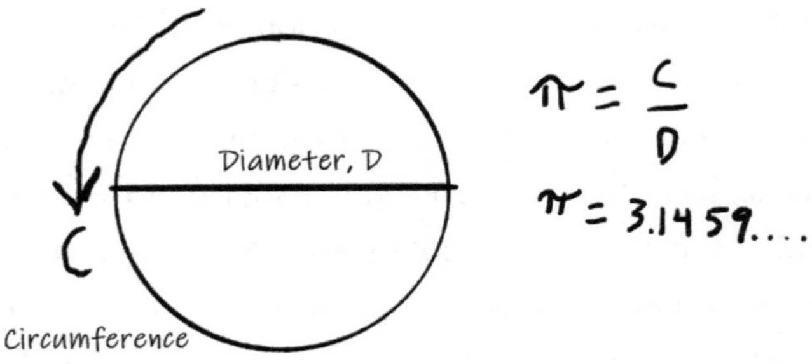

The path of a circle continues round and round infinitely if we keep on tracing it. Even though this path never stops, it's boring, because we know where it starts, where it stops, and how it travels. A never-ending cycle with these parameters can be a description of hell, an infinite loop. Yet we know so much about this circle, or any circle. How can we not stop it? We know its diameter, and can calculate its entire length, its circumference, with this number Pi. But Pi is an infinitely long and complex number. It can represent the randomness of life, the infinite number of variables that manifest as a life is lived. You cannot predict it. You cannot control it. How do you stop Pi? You stop Pi as you would any form of "this or that": you view it as a bounded paradox.

Anger is the opposite of fear, as we saw in Chapter 2. Anger is the condition whereby one might confront something or explode from a situation; fear is the condition whereby one might shy away from something or implode from a situation. Anger tends to provoke action. Fear tends to produce inaction or flight from the fearful situation.

I could bore you with an infinite number of other examples. I'm sure you can think of many yourself. What does this all mean? It means that thinking is based on a sort of logic that compares two or more things and chooses yes or no in response to this process. Sometimes, the output isn't a mere yes or no, but a selection from a finite or infinite set of things, but it's still concluded with: "Is this the best decision? Yes." The final outcome is always binary, a 1 or a 0. If the answer were never a 1, no one would ever do or choose anything. Saying "Yes, this is acceptable" is what stops the rumination about what to do, what to choose, what to say, or how to act. There are a lot of details that happen between these points, and we will discuss them, but for now, let's discuss "this or that."

RIGHT AND WRONG

After a decision is contemplated, once its outcome is safely in the past, we like to label it as a "good" or "bad" decision. While we say hindsight is 20/20, this label is based upon a very subjective interpretation of the outcome. Remember, 20/20 vision is just "average," and judging something only in hindsight is exactly what the average person does. What's good for one person may not be good for another person. But, we all know the difference between good and bad, don't we? Good is this, and bad is that. Or is it bad is this, and good is that? Questions of morality, and how to answer them, span infinitely. People don't realize this and it causes all kinds of trouble. You will often hear someone say, "I know what is right, and I know what is wrong." How do you know though? How do you *really know?*

There is religion to guide us in what is right and what is wrong. A good example is the Ten Commandments from the Book of Exodus. A secular group of laws, predating Exodus, is Hammurabi's Code. The most famous edict of Hammurabi's Code is "an eye for an eye ," which means if someone punches you in the face, they should be punched in the face. A witty response to "an eye for an eye" is, "an eye for an eye makes the world go blind." This witty response actually has two meanings. It means that if people keep reciprocating damage that is based on the damage inflicted, the damage will continue indefinitely. Another meaning is that this "eye for an eye" philosophy blinds the world to proper morality, law, and ethics.

The New Testament proclaimed the most famous, simplest, and maybe best guidance on how to act: Do to others as you would have them do to you. -Luke 6:31. This concept is so important that it is mentioned in many other Bible verses. This guidance works well for relatively simple things, like refraining from insulting someone because you would prefer not to be insulted. Or, don't steal something from someone because you'd rather not have your stuff stolen. Don't cheat on your girlfriend because you wouldn't like it if she cheated on you. But what about this: give advice when someone needs it because you'd like it if someone gave advice to you when you needed it. There's a problem here, because a dichotomy could exist between those who need advice and those who don't. This example could flip to *don't give me advice I don't need because I would prefer not to receive advice I don't need.* One person could think someone needs advice, and that person could disagree. Complicating things further, a person could need advice but not want it given unless they asked for it first. The golden rule fails here because it is too simple, and does not take into account that individuals may interpret situations differently. A polite person would take the unsolicited advice with a grain of salt, and offer thanks. They may feel slightly abased that someone else thought they needed help when they thought they didn't, but they wouldn't express this to the advice giver. Good manners would smooth over the mistake made by using the Golden Rule. It is said that "manners are the glue of society." They are what keep us together.

Manners aren't enough, however. A moral compass is necessary to navigate more complicated scenarios. The reason why it's called a moral compass is because a compass needle always tries to face the same way, but rotating the compass in different directions causes the needle to move and it has to balance back to pointing north. Challenging situations cause changes in viewpoints, positions, variables, and the availability of information. Therefore, one's moral compass may bounce around quite a bit. Some people's moral compasses settle quicker than others, because they tend to know where their true north is. These are the people who know exactly what to do when a tricky situation presents itself (at least morally speaking).

Here is a complicated choice based upon hypothetical considerations of morality. It is easy to pretend this is a real-life situation. Imagine that two people need a heart transplant: a three-year-old girl from a poor family and a sixty-five-year-old scientist who happens to be a Nobel Laureate. Only one heart is available for the transplant, and the person who does not receive it is certain to die. Who should get the heart? This kind of decision is where weighting, factors, and weighting factors come into play. Along with these comes a moral compass. Each choice and weighting is still on that spectrum of this or that. For example, a formula for determining who gets the transplant could be a score derived from something like this, and whoever receives the higher score gets the heart:

Score = (Years of Life Left) * (Quality of Life) + (Years of Life Left) * (Number of Contributions to Society per Year) + (Unknown Potential for Good) – (Unknown Potential for Bad)

Determining this score requires a great deal of subjectivity, but this formula entails the reasoning that would be present in determining who should receive the transplant. The three-year-old has many years of life left, but the quality and societal contribution of that life is uncertain. The scientist has fewer years left, but is likely to have a high quality of life during those years and may contribute another great thing to society (like something worthy of another Nobel Prize). It is also unknown how many contributions to society per year the child will make, after he or she is older. The scientist will probably make a countable number of contributions to society per year. On the other hand, the scientist may retire and may not make any more scientific contributions to society. The Potential for Good and Bad is a life assessment. This is how this person's life affected people, how many people loved them, and how many people they loved. This is probably known for the scientist, but unknown for the child. We can assume the child is an average person, so these two factors would cancel each other out.

There is one thing the child would get from the transplant that the scientist could not. This is not reflected in the score. This is the chance to complete the score starting from near the beginning of life. For the scientist, the score is mostly complete, and there is little left to chance. One could say, "Give it to the child, because they deserve a chance at eighty years of life." The scientist would most likely live only another fifteen years. So eighty years are granted by giving the heart to the child, and the scientist loses fifteen years, so there is a net gain of sixty-five years. Sixty-five years of life are determined to be enough for the scientist in order to give the child a chance to live a full lifespan. The scientist loses 15 years. So, there is a net gain of 65 years. The child should probably get the transplant.

Now, I mentioned that the child comes from a poor family. Because of this, the likelihood of their having a great life is lower than average. The impact of the decision could only be seen and evaluated to be correct if both choices were allowed to play out, and could be observed and measured for the duration of the lives of both people. Even then, a fair amount of judgment would be required to compute the score. In society, potential tends to be viewed as greater than actualization. Actualization is "you had your chance and did this." Potential is "you have the potential to do this or that." A number-one draft pick excites people more than the Hall of Fame inductee. We are afraid of the unknown, but it excites us and we love it.

So what happened here? The formula for the score was too

complicated, so the number of years of life was substituted in order to make a decision. The number-of-years method appeals to everyone and is much simpler to articulate. People make decisions and think like this all the time. If a problem or concept is too hard, it gets simplified with assumptions, and then solved.

Here is another illustration of the slippery concept of right and wrong. It is common for a divorcee to say something like, "My biggest regret is having met my ex." But, quickly, they catch themselves and add, "But that's not true, because if I hadn't met my ex, I wouldn't have had Bobby and Ricky." This simple statement certainly expresses love for her children, but it's erasing the potential of an entire life stream that could have taken place if the she had not met her ex. But that potential comprises years of decisions, cause and effect, probabilities, being in the right place at the right or wrong time—it's the ripple in the water caused by the plunking of the rock. It's impossible to imagine the complexities, the changes, and how life would have ended up had that one decision gone the other way.

This is true of many single decisions in life. The divorcee would never have known Bobby and Ricky if she hadn't met her ex; therefore, she could not regret not having had them. So, as painful as it is to imagine the nonexistence of two known children, the statement is patently false. It is impossible for this divorcee to know if she actually regrets meeting her ex. Indeed, we can think of many good things, unintended consequences, happy accidents, and the like, that have resulted from our regrets. This is one of the reasons people should have no regrets. Because, in the end, the consequences of a regretful decision being erased or reversed could result in a better situation than the existing one. What's more, it could create a better stream of events leading to the present than the current one. However, it is possible that if each stream and situation were evaluated perfectly they could be exactly equal. After it is accepted that:

This = That

this is the exact conclusion that one would arrive at.

THIS IS THAT

The yin-yang symbol shows the perfect mixing of the forces of yin and yang. Yang is the powerful, light, male force. Yin is the feminine, dark, hidden force. Figure 3-1 shows the symbol of the yin-yang symbol.

Figure 3-1: the Yin-Yang Symbol

One of the things most people don't notice about this symbol is the small black dot in the white and the small white dot in the black. This is consistent with the division between the black and white being a curved border. What these dots are saying is that there is a little bit of yin in yang and vice versa. This statement isn't that profound when talking about mysterious Chinese forces, but when applied to more common concepts, it resolves the conflict of categorizing things as this or that, true or false, black or white, good or bad, ugly or beautiful, and so on. "It's a gray area," people say. Or, more extreme, people say, "Everything is gray." Everything is gray, and the shade of gray is dependent on the tint of the glasses we are wearing when we look at each thing.

For every true statement, there is a little bit of a lie to it. For every false statement, there is a little bit of truth to it. Every good person is a little bad, and every bad person is a little good. A felon on death row is probably still loved by his mother or at least one other person, even though society has condemned him to death and he is generally hated by everyone. With light and dark, one can only know dark because of light. Light has different intensities, so there is darkness in every beam of light. Similarly, there is nothing that is absolutely dark; a little bit of light exists in even pitch darkness. What we have here is a paradox. Two things that are opposites are actually somewhat the same. With the proper knowledge, we can bind this paradox with our minds and accept it.

BOUNDED PARADOXES

Here is another symbol you might have seen. It's the Freemason symbol. I will not tell you what the Freemasons say it means, because I am bound not to disclose any Freemasonry secrets to any people who are not Freemasons. However, I came up with this interpretation before I became a Freemason, and the Lodge never stated my definition. Therefore, I am permitted to share it with you. Figure 3-2 is the Freemasonry symbol I am referring to.

Figure 3-2: Freemasonry Square and Compass Symbol

I want you to recall the earlier discussion of how a straight line and a circle or curved line are related to each other. A compass is used to draw perfect circles. If you've never used one, you simply anchor one point, and spin the other point around the stationary one to make a circle. The farther from each other the points are, or the wider you open the compass, the larger the circle becomes. If you open up the compass completely, the compass becomes a line. If you connect the two ends of the completely open compass, the result is a straight line. If a compass of a certain size is made, and you know its size, you can create a line of a known size by connecting its points with the square. If you close the compass completely, the two points intersect, and you can create a circle with a diameter of zero, or a single point. In geometry, a point is defined as a location marker that is infinitely small, or infinitesimal. It has no dimensions in any direction. If one possessed a compass whose points where infinitely small, one could create a point as defined in geometry.

Let's consider the square, the right-angled bottom (in the Freemasonry symbol) measuring and marking tool. A square is two rulers that intersect at a right angle. Notice on the square above that the edges are rounded, and the graduations are incomplete. This is indicating that the length of the square goes on infinitely. In geometry, we also learn that a circle with a radius of zero is two lines at right angles to each other, which is an angle of 90 degrees. Using this knowledge, we see that the square, which is used to draw straight lines, can be looked at as a circle. The square can be used as a simple ruler to measure the diameter of a circle. Once the diameter of a circle is known, its circumference can be determined by multiplying its diameter by the number Pi. Or, one could use the compass: spread the two points at a distance of half the diameter, and draw a circle of the intended size. The knowledge of Pi is not necessary. As we said before, a circle with an infinite radius has a completely straight surface. Conversely, if the diameter of the circle is measured with an infinitely small measurement, a straight line is the result (this is the same as making the circle infinitely large). Finally, if you take a square, and make points of equal length on both sides of the square from its edges, along its graduations, and then place it on a surface and spin it, you will create a circle with a diameter that is known without taking a direct measurement. The familiar Pythagorean Theorem can be used to determine the hypotenuse of the square, which is the longer length created between the two "rules" that have a set measurement. The Pythagorean Theorem is:

$$a^2 + b^2 = c^2$$

$$c = \sqrt{a^2 + b^2}$$

$$c = \sqrt{1^2 + 1^2} = \sqrt{2}$$

Geometrically, this looks like this:

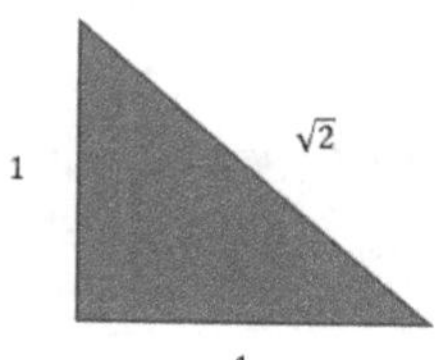

Figure 3-3: Right Triangle with Legs of Equal Length

Note that the Pythagorean Theorem is only applicable to right triangles—that is, triangles with one internal angle of 90 degrees. The legs do not have to be of equal length. So the diameter of a circle with a measurement of 7 on both sides of the square would be the square root of 7 squared plus 7 squared, which is equal to 9.899... If anyone is interested in proving this, take a square and perform the procedure. If a square is not available, align two rulers as close to 90 degrees as possible, and do the same thing. What's more, if the angle between the two compass arms is known, and the length of each compass arm is known, the distance between the compass points can be determined by a more general form of the Pythagorean Theorem. Or, if the angle between the two compass arms is known as well as the length of the circle's radius, the length of each compass arm can be determined.

The G in the middle of the Square and Compass symbol, Figure 3-2, symbolizes either geometry, God, or both. The full understanding of geometry, as described above, illuminates the observer to the fact that a circle and a line can be thought of as the same thing, even though they are different. Geometry is knowing everything that is seen, and all of the relationships between the elements that constitute the observed geometry. God is symbolized by geometry, because God knows everything about all the geometry of the universe. This is sometimes symbolized by the all-seeing eye, which sometimes appears within or above the Square and Compass Symbol. A more generalized version of the all-seeing eye can be seen in *Figure 3-4* below, in its most famous version on the one-dollar bill.

Figure 3-4: the All Seeing Eye on the One Dollar Bill

The G symbolizes what you may be able to see now. I like the term "bounded paradox." A "bounded paradox" is different than a simple paradox. A simple paradox is an inkling that two things are different but related. A "bounded paradox" is when all of the relationships between the paradoxical elements are known, understood, and accepted. Binding paradoxes are a necessary path to serenity, tranquility, and wisdom. Bounded paradoxes are the essence of reality, and a glimpse at the Truth. The universe is an infinite spectrum of an infinite number of bounded paradoxes. For example, the gravity within a black hole is infinite; the gravity in free fall orbit in outer space is zero.

CHAPTER 4: TRUTH, FALSEHOOD, AND LIES

What someone thinks is the truth is the ultimate determinator of what they think is right or wrong, good or bad, worthwhile or a waste of time. It is the backdrop behind someone making an assessment, a judgment, or indeed, any decision. If someone believes that if they lived a good life here on earth they will go to heaven when they die, they will strive to live a good life here on earth to realize that reward. If someone believes they've already been sentenced to Hell and no redemption is possible, they will act accordingly: either continue to act bad or effect as much good as possible to decrease the level of punishment in hell.

What is truth, though? *That's a stupid question. The truth is something that is true.* Well, now we're using a word to define itself. According to dictionary.com, here are the definitions of "truth":

1. the true or actual state of a matter
2. conformity with fact or reality; verity

3. a verified or indisputable fact, proposition, principle, or the like
4. the state or character of being true
5. actuality or actual existence
6. an obvious or accepted fact; truism; platitude

These definitions are pretty boring upon a cursory review, but as we examine each definition, truth seems to lose its foundation. Definition 1 does the same thing I did above; it uses the same word to define itself. In definition 2, we can remember that facts change and are arbitrary, and what is reality has been debated for a long time. Remember when Pluto was a planet and there were only four oceans? Again, in definition 3, the term indisputable comes into question. OJ was found to be innocent. Definition 4 again defines itself with the same word. Number 5 refers to existence, which is merely a representation in reality—the pesky question of reality springs up again. Definition 6 shows that truth is based on popular opinion and a classification of what is obvious and what is not. Whether someone is happy or sad is not obvious to a person with autism. Truth is a sort of popularity contest. In the movie *12 Monkeys,* Jeffrey Goines, played by Brad Pitt, states it perfectly:

Jeffrey Goines: There's no right, there's no wrong, there's only popular opinion.

THE TRUTH OF PAST REALITY

Jeffrey also makes the point that until recently, germs "did not exist." People who believed in them were deemed crazy. The same thing was thought about atoms when they were being discovered in the 1900s. At the risk of quoting too many movies, there's another good framing of truth in the movie *Memento.* The main character in this movie, Leonard, has a special type of amnesia where he can only remember the past before a certain point, when he sustained a brain injury. After the injury, he cannot make new memories and lives in ten-minute windows, after which he forgets them forever. This is a real condition, and is caused by the removal or damage of the hippocampi, which are the structures in the brain that permit the brain to transfer short term memories into long term memories. Reflecting upon his condition, having no short-term memory, Leonard says:

You know the truth about my condition, officer? You don't know anything.

You feel angry, you don't know why. You feel guilty, you have no idea why.

You could do anything and not have the faintest idea ten minutes later.

Leonard is saying he doesn't know what's true because he can't sync his emotions up to the reality that's in the past. In his last statement, he's saying that he can no longer observe cause and effect, which is actually the element that directs time's arrow to begin with (effects are not observed before their causes)[12].

So now, we have three candidates for truth: popular opinion, remembering what happened or what caused an emotion or feeling, and cause and effect in general. All three of these candidates can be shaken down, and are unacceptable definitions for truth.

In order to get at truth, we would have to know, in totality, what is. In order to know what is, we have to know what was.

---

12 https://en.wikipedia.org/wiki/Arrow_of_time

As in, what is reality, what exactly caused this situation, why is this person a certain way, and all of these things to the greatest extent possible back to the origin of the universe, the Big Bang. Examining yourself, you can say that you are the totality of your experiences—that is to say, your memories. Your memories are an interpretation of what happened during your life experience. When you were a baby, for whatever reason, there was no way to make this interpretation, or store it, so you don't remember anything, and neither does anyone else. Many people think that memory is like a tape recorder that records their entire life. When pressed to remember a situation, event, or fact, they can become very touchy and exclaim, "That's the way it was. I remember!" For people who study memory or neuroscience, or rely on eyewitness testimony, they know that memory is extremely unreliable. Not only that, but also that about 90 to 95 percent of what we experience gets almost perfectly forgotten. So, sadly, if an eighty-year-old could play his or her life on a video screen, we would only get eight years of footage. In other words, memory is not a beholder of truth.

The collection of events, decisions, variables, weather, and other chaotic factors that crystalized your memories, which later melted, have branches of explanation that extend billions of years into the past. Take your own genetic makeup. This is the product of billions of years of evolution, lovers' choices, and the life conditions of your lineage. Epigenetics[13] is a new sub-field of genetics that suggests that genes are influenced by a lifetime preceding, or even a couple of generations before, new genes are created. The conditions that existed just a few generations before you crafted the epigenetics that were used as the final tweak to create you when you were just a zygote. I'll tell you the truth:

13 https://ghr.nlm.nih.gov/primer/howgeneswork/epigenome

to know what is, in its totality, one has to know everything that has happened up until that point. This is impossible for anyone, except for a Supreme Being. Only the Supreme Being knows what is becausewhat is is almost totally dependent upon the past.

THE TRUTH OF REALITY YET TO COME

Many statements concerning truth are dependent on what happens in the future. They are not proven to be true or false until that event unfolds. A weather prediction is a simple example of this. A weather prediction is made, that day comes, and we can then judge whether the weatherman's prediction was true, or we can say the weatherman prediction was right. Truth can dictate right and wrong, and, conversely, right and wrong can dictate the truth. The meteorologist doesn't give a certainty to her predictions, but this serves as an example.

"I will clean the house tomorrow." This statement will be proven true or false in the future. Even if this was prevented by an emergency or other legitimate reason, it still becomes a falsehood if it doesn't happen. However, to know the veracity of the statement when it's made, one needs to know what will happen in the future.

People express the understandable desire to be judged not by their actions or how they turn out (which we have less control over), but rather by their intent in choosing these actions. We can control our intent much better than our actions and the outcome of them. When the person fails to clean the house, they will say something like, "I had every intention of cleaning the house today, but my boss called me and asked me to complete a last minute project. I had to get this done, and I wasn't left with enough time to clean the house." The truthfulness of this statement can be shown by the work product that was completed, the one assigned by the boss at the last minute. What we don't know is whether she would have cleaned the house if it hadn't been for the boss. When she says "I had every intention..." we can't judge this statement unless we are mind readers.

Many more examples can be given of how truth depends on future events. "It was the best possible decision." This can't be known unless, again, multiple universes or perfect simulations of every decision available were made and then were evaluated with perfect judgment, weighting all factors perfectly, and then coming to a conclusion of which decision was the best. The conclusion may be, impossibly, that all decisions were equal. This may be hard to imagine, but consider the length of time the impact of a decision is felt. This is related to the regret of the divorcees back in Chapter 3. If you throw a number of rocks into a pond, the ripples caused by each rock will eventually settle and the pond will be the same as it was, regardless of each rock thrown.

ABSOLUTE TRUTH

The conclusion is that the entire past, all aspects of the present condition, and the future all have to be known in order to know "what is." Moving the present condition to any moment of time, truth is simply "what is," at any given moment, considering the past and future before and after that moment. It's always the present, so the truth is always knowing "what is."

For a limited being, there is no such thing as truth. There are only limited perspectives that are accepted or rejected in order to make decisions, come to action, stop an action, lead a train of thought further, stop a train of thought, or divert a train of thought. It is the same as a belief, except the person holding it elevates it to a higher level of importance than a belief, because they think it mirrors reality.

Even if you could see everything that is, that was, and ever will be simultaneously, you would merely see it. You would see is, was and will be. It wouldn't be true or false, unless you knew that there wasn't a total state called isn't. Then is would be true and isn't would be false. However, in order to verify isn't, something that is would have to be, a necessary observer, and that would violate the definition of isn't. Therefore, proving isn't is impossible, and you can't say is is true or false. The condition of "isn't" is one of a single being experiencing a perspective unified by a single consciousness, or perspective, with a world imagined and known by this single consciousness. It would be like a child playing a pretend game where they play the part of every character, construct the playset, and determine how long to play. The condition of isn't is before the universe was created and after it ends. It is the child before and after she plays pretend. It is John 1:1, "In the beginning was the Word, and the Word was with God, and the Word was God." This cryptic bible verse will be explained later in this book.

For us mortals, truth is a belief based on available evidence. It is used to influence our thoughts, emotions, actions, and intentions. The knowledge of absolute truth would prevent one from making a decision, because all of the infinite variables and influences would probably balance out. Ironically, ff this was known, decision certainty, based on total truth, would be less concrete. People would be more likely to change their minds, and more empathy would be possible. The absolute conviction of right or wrong based on truths leads to destruction, war, hatred, and many other damaging things. It is the doubt of one's truth that leads to changed perspectives, compromises, resolution of conflicts, and many positive things. This is the ultimate "benefit of the doubt."

In the Bible, assuming perfect knowledge of truth, which leads to an absolute conviction or so-called knowledge of what's right or wrong, is latent. It is the eating of the tree of the knowledge of good and evil from which, reflexively, all evil manifests. In Genesis 2:17, it is stated:

But of the tree of the knowledge of good and evil, thou shalt not eat of it: for in the day that thou eatest thereof thou shalt surely die.

Adam and Eve do eat of the fruit, and they don't die. In fact, that's one of the truths the serpent tells Eve to convince her to eat from the tree to begin with. What dies is their innocence, an egoless mind, and a conviction that they knew better. An ego, a false self, is born, at the expense of the true self, which does not consider anything thing good or bad, or any one thing true or false. It is the death of this true self that God was referring to. The serpent was referring to a physical death, and was also telling the truth. So, here we are in Genesis, with God and Satan saying the same thing, and both of them were telling the truth. Truth is all about perspective.

FALSEHOOD

Falsehood may sometimes be likened to lies, but it is different. Lies carry selfish intentions. Falsehood is merely the condition of what isn't, what wasn't, and what won't be. In order to know total falsehood, one needs to know everything that is, and subtract what is thought, supposed, or promised. Where:

Falsehood = All that is possible – What was – What is – What will be

Falsehood exists when someone makes an inaccurate prediction. Their prediction is false, which is proven by the actualization of an unpredicted future. Falsehood is when someone believes something happened in the past when it actually didn't. Falsehood is an incorrect answer to a concrete math problem. The "False" statement is commonly used in computer programs to instruct the program what to do. The false statement always follows an "if" statement and the "then" statement is always after the "false" condition. Here is an example:

If x > 10 is false, then display "x is less than 10." Where x is any number.

Considering our universe, and not many universes, or the multiverse, there are a greater number of falsehoods than truths. This is because the definition of falsehood includes "All that is possible," which is pretty much everything. Falsehood is not bad. It is something used to determine a pretty good truth, which is the best we can ever do. A falsehood can be equated to anything we can imagine that never actually happened or that will happen.

LIES

We all know what a lie is, and the definition and exposition here is basically a formality and is necessary for the precise definitions, knowledge, and relationships that emotions, concepts, thoughts, and feelings are intertwined with.

Lies are basically things that are told, shown, not shown, not told, withheld, made prominent, and the like in an effort to make things more convenient, possible, probable, less severe, easier, or more sympathetic for the liar. The quickest definition is that a lie is "something crafted to make things more convenient for someone." They are basically shortcuts. They are shortcuts that come at a price, though. Research shows that lies come at the expense of extra mental effort and stressful biometrics. We would all like things to be easier and more convenient. This explains why lies are so prominent. Lies also highlight falsehood that is known, and shadows that what is thought to be true. Sympathetic lies are the so-called "white lies" that are designed to protect the feelings of others.

The tricky thing about lies, which are already tricky, is that they can become true under a shift of perspective. For example, I tell my children that Santa Claus is real, which is a white lie, because it makes Christmas more exciting for them. The role of Santa Claus has been played by my wife and me for many years. I eventually tell my children that "Santa Claus" is not real. They accuse me of lying, which is true from a certain standpoint. I can counter with "Actually, your parents are Santa Claus, because we fulfill all of the acts that Santa performs, and we know when you've been bad or good so be good for goodness sake just like the song says." Santa Claus was just an imaginative disguise, and a convention used by many, so we only need to be exonerated for donning a secret identity in the same fashion that a superhero would. This imaginative, yet truthful, perspective on Santa Claus completely changes negative feelings towards the Santa Claus reveal. And besides, Mom and Dad would rather get credit for putting on the Christmas event, wouldn't they?

A lot of people brag about always "telling the truth," or "I have no filter." These are the people who would tell you that your outfit is terrible, that you shouldn't talk so much, or that you deserved to get fired from your job. These are all accurate statements, but they are painful things to hear. Someone with good manners would tell white lies during these occasions, out of sympathy. The intention of lies is what determines their possibility for positive or negative outcomes. Of course, even a white lie can have negative consequences. A friend may have knowledge that her friend's husband is cheating on her. She withholds the knowledge because it would devastate her friend. She can't bear to be the messenger of bad news. After the affair is exposed and she becomes aware that her friend had known, she could very well be angry at her friend for not disclosing it. Did her friend make the right choice? Was the cheating victim justified in her anger? I don't know. And neither of them knows either, because the decision and the reaction were based on emotions or feelings and other factors. Emotions are reflexive, so we can't judge based on them. However, feelings are emotions that are pondered, considered, and stewed upon over a period of time. If we act out of feelings, those feelings and the resulting actions can be evaluated or judged.

It is also possible to lie to take a shortcut or make things more convenient for you without damaging someone else. If a student cheats on a test, it doesn't really hurt the other students, but it causes an unfair condition. If this condition is never known by anyone, it doesn't hurt anyone or disrupt their moral compass. The person cheating is damaging themselves, because they failed to learn the material the exam was based on. Eventually, when the cheater can't cheat and has to take the exam legitimately, they will not know what they would have learned had they not cheated on the other tests, and they will fail that test and future tests.

Ultimately, lies are merely a method of delaying something that is expected to be unpleasant or until you are in a better condition to perform or deal with it. I receive a call late in the day from a client who would like to spend thirty minutes talking about their project. I don't feel it's the best time to discuss the project, given my fatigue. I could tell the client this, but I don't think they would appreciate my not feeling like talking to them.

Or, I could say that I am not in the office, but I could talk to them early the following day. What did I just do? I delayed the effort of having to talk to them about their project to a time that was more convenient for me. The time may not have been as convenient for them, or they may have wanted to discuss their project right when they called me. So there could be a cost to them for my lie. However, I could justify my lie by illustrating the fact that they probably should have scheduled the phone call to begin with. Be prepared to justify lying to delay effort or suspend something unpleasant, because hidden costs may accrue in the meantime.

CHAPTER 5: BECOMING COMFORTABLE WITH ANXIETY

Anxiety is the most common mental illness and probably the most common negative, plaguing feeling people endure every day. Medication, psychotherapy, and counseling can alleviate the symptoms of anxiety, but they rarely, if ever, completely cure it, because the source of the anxiety is never addressed.

The source is never found because there are so many different types of anxiety, and the focus is misplaced on the settings, the triggers, and the resulting feelings—instead of on the source. Anxiety was defined in Chapter 2. It's a lingering fear, without an identifiable cause, that something bad is going to happen. There are normally certain conditions or variables that trigger or increase feelings of anxiety, but the reasons why they do this are unknown to the sufferer.

Certain Situation or Setting→Anxiety

As Duration of Certain Situations or Settings ↑ the Feelings of Anxiety ↑

Anxiety is when someone feels vulnerable and uncomfortable. Sometimes people feel this way all the time. Sometimes anxiety morphs into Obsessive Compulsive Disorder, a condition related to anxiety, whereby a person performs rituals completes actions, or thinks thoughts repeatedly in a certain sequence, to alleviate the feelings of anxiety. Anxiety and OCD can become so overwhelming and pervasive that they can eventually lead to suicide.

THE SOURCE OF ANXIETY

The ultimate source of anxiety is the fear or inability to accept the loss of self, forms of self, shades of self, and life in general. The ultimate source of anxiety is the knowledge of death. Kids don't really have anxiety. Kids don't really ponder their mortality or worry too much about being injured by playing, taking risks, and doing other things that adults don't normally do. I have experienced a great deal of anxiety in my life, and certain forms of OCD. When suffering from anxiety, the sufferer knows deep down that the fear is unreasonable or unfounded, but they feel it anyway. I will illustrate with some real examples how ridiculous anxiety can be. OCD is one of the worse forms of torture. It glues you to a certain series of thoughts or behavior, and prevents you from living your life.

THE RECEDING HAIRLINE

As I was growing older, I couldn't help but notice how I was aging. I noticed lines on my face that weren't there before, I had gained weight, I wasn't as flexible, and so on. Something made me think about male balding, and I imagined how I would feel if I went bald. I would feel very old. Then something reminded me that an early sign of balding was a receding hairline. I immediately went to the mirror to inspect my hairline to see if it had receded. Initially, I didn't compare it with anything. I just inspected it to see if it resembled a receding hairline. I did this repeatedly and didn't find any signs of a receding hairline, but my inspection didn't satisfy me. I found an older picture of myself and compared it to my reflection. I did this repeatedly, but the anxiety wouldn't go away. I stopped inspecting my hairline, but the obsession continued after that. Eventually, I started asking people if I had a receding hairline or if my hairline had receded since I was younger. The embarrassment of asking such a silly question did little to stop me from asking. The people I asked said either "No," or "Maybe just a little bit." The worry and anxiety over this eventually faded away.

Why did I have this anxiety? It was because I couldn't accept the possibility of going bald, having a receding hairline, or looking prematurely older. This was because I noticed I was starting to look older. The evidence of aging made me feel vulnerable. I had to realize the boundaries of aging, and try to smudge or erase them. I had to at least smudge them from my observations.

THE FIRE THAT NEVER BURNED THE CATS AND THE BEDBUGS THAT NEVER CAME

I had a friend who was troubled by a high degree of general anxiety and some OCD-like symptoms. Her biggest problem was leaving the house. She was afraid to leave the house, because she was afraid that something would catch fire while she was gone.

She wasn't so afraid of a fire in general, but that a fire would most likely harm or kill her cats. She lived alone, and her cats were very dear to her. So her routine of leaving the house would consist of the following:

- Checking the curling iron ten times to ensure it was both turned off and unplugged. At its worst, this would result in staring at the empty receptacle and repeating "off, off, off..."

- Checking the stove burners, even though she never cooked, to ensure they were all turned off. This check would also take some time.

- She had placed extra carbon monoxide and smoke detectors throughout her apartment to ensure a carbon monoxide leak from the furnace wouldn't kill anyone.

- All appliances on the kitchen counters were turned off and unplugged.

- The locks were locked and relocked multiple times.

- Sometimes, after she finally left, she wasn't sure of what she had checked, so she would drive back to her house to check again, just to be sure, on her way to work. It made her late a couple of times.

I have knowledge of fire and electrical safety, so I would explain the various protective features that were intrinsic to her modern electrical wiring system, appliances, and HVAC equipment. I explained to her how certain appliances were designed with various safety measures to prevent fires and injuries. Finally, I told her that most house fires were from cooking. As I said, she didn't cook, so I told her she didn't have anything to worry about. This technical knowledge allayed her fears somewhat, but she was pretty smart, and her mind would eventually concoct various other scenarios to worry about. She just wanted her cats to be safe. Eventually, she developed a fear of bedbugs that was triggered by another bad situation in her life. When her anxiety became untenable, she would call me and I would help calm her down. I had personal experience with anxiety, OCD, and craziness, so she trusted me as a resource.

The source of the anxiety about her cats is obvious. She couldn't bear to lose the cats in an accident or situation that could have been prevented. She wouldn't be able to forgive herself. A faux mountain produced by certain life possibilities is what causes anxiety. This woman really valued comfort, consistency, and security. If her home became infested with bedbugs, the process of getting rid of them would completely ruin the sanctuary of her house. This is why the bedbugs became an obsession and a source of anxiety.

THE PLANE CRASHING INTO MY HOUSE

I remember the very first time I experienced acute anxiety. I also remember knowing that it was ridiculous. I was so embarrassed by it that I never went to anyone for help, so I suffered in silence. This is in stark contrast to my son, who now confesses all of his anxieties to me, and listens to me carefully as I explain to him why he need not worry about it. Maybe I should have done that when I was younger.

I was about thirteen years old. I had never flown in a plane before, and if given the chance to avoid it, I would have. I guess the news reports and movies of plane crashes scared me. Car accidents are common, but they are not always fatal. Most plane crashes involve fatalities and many kill everyone on board. That's the scary thing about them. When they crash, there is a total loss.

Somehow, it also occurred to me that when planes crash, they can also crash into things. They can crash into things like trees, buildings, and houses. So, even though I'm not riding on a plane, what if one were to crash into my house and kill everybody?[14] This event, while possible, was so improbable, who would ever worry about it? I did. I worried about it every time I went to bed, and every time I heard a plane pass over my house. I don't know if my senses were just better then, the house I lived in had loose construction and I could more easily hear sounds from outside, or if the house I grew up in was closer to major plane routes. In any event, in a given night, I could hear quite a few planes flying by distantly. Every time I heard one, I would brace myself, and I would wait for signs that the plane was on its way to crash into my house. This went on for months, and my nights were filled with terror. I didn't sleep well. I didn't tell a soul about my fear, because I knew it was stupid and I didn't want to appear crazy or stupid.

I don't recall how the plane crash fear finally went away. I remember when it did go away, it was final, and I never was afraid of it again. I started sleeping peacefully at night. This fear, and the resulting anxiety, was caused by the risk of something having an infinite magnitude of consequences. The definition of risk is:

Risk = Probability of Event x Consequence of Event

If the mind is calculating a risk, it can estimate probability to a reasonable degree. However, the consequences of events are very emotional and definitive, and the magnitude of a consequence of an event can approach the infinite. Because of this, highly improbable events become risky events. Risky events that are present cause fear. Fear that is constantly associated

14 Incidentally, one of the movies I later became obsessed with, *Donnie Darko,* actually featured the main character getting killed by a jet engine that fell from a plane.

with certain risks evolves into anxiety. The only ways to reduce the risk and reduce the anxiety are to reduce the magnitude of the consequence of an event or realize the improbability of it happening. Another way to reduce the anxiety is to accept the risk. In most cases, this involves accepting the possibility of losing oneself partially or totally, losing a loved one, becoming homeless, losing a partner (through divorce or otherwise), or something happening to one's kid. Most anxieties are over losing yourself. It extends so far that people get super anxious around people who are sick because they don't want to go through the uncomfortable ordeal of having a cold, or maybe they are afraid that the cold will seriously jeopardize their health.

CONTRACTING AIDS IN HIGH SCHOOL

I went through the standard health class in high school that educates students in sexual education, health, and, of course, sexually transmitted diseases. The diseases like gonorrhea and chlamydia or even syphilis didn't faze me at all. They are completely curable, and only do harm if left unchecked long term. Genital warts were definitely intrinsically unattractive, and they bothered me because they never went away. Then, insidiously, HIV and AIDS were discussed. I was in this class around the mid-90s. HIV wasn't a quick death sentence as it was when it first broke out in the early 80s, but it was still a death sentence. This scared me unimaginably.

I was moderately sexually active when I learned about HIV. Immediately after, whenever I had a new sexual encounter, I was afraid. *"What if she had HIV and I just got it?"* Again, I knew the chances were so slim that they probably couldn't even be computed, but I worried about it nonetheless. I worried about other

STDs too, and about contracting them. I remember asking girls, before partaking in any sexual activity, and they asked me the same thing: "You don't have any STDs, do you?"

Back then, if a girl had sex with three of four different guys, I thought she was too promiscuous, and wouldn't date her, lest she infect me with an STD. Other boys felt the same way. One friend realized the stupidity of that logic. He was a fan of the TV Show *Seinfeld,* and he reasoned something like this: "People who date in adult life up into their 30s probably end up sleeping with thirty or forty people, yet they aren't super worried about STDs all the time. I don't know why we are." His words were prophetic, because I did date in my 30s after I got divorced, and some people in the dating arena certainly slept with that many people and more. As an adult, I didn't think twice about sleeping with them or contracting STDs. The risks that were associated with STDs presented in high school were overblown, probably on purpose. HIV never became the heterosexual killer it was predicted to be. Now, HIV is portrayed with people running in fields and laughing at ballgames in advertisements for the latest HIV medications. My friend bringing up the adult dating trends was the mechanism of logic that often reduces or eradicates certain causes of anxiety. Training your mind to methodically evaluate the risks that produce anxiety is one method of reducing it.

As Logic ↑ Anxiety ↓

The two prerequisites for using logic to reduce anxiety are increased knowledge about the risk, and a rational use of logic to further evaluate the anxiety caused by the risk. The knowledge can come in the form of statistics, new observations, consultation with a more knowledgeable person, or more life experience. Logical thinking develops from formal education, applying general reasoning to normal problems, and stifling emotions when employing this type of thinking.

Here is an extreme example of using statistics, reasoning, and even computation in an effort to alleviate anxiety. My AIDS obsession was so pervasive and enduring that I made a spreadsheet to calculate the chances that I would ever contract it. I never got tested for it until many years later. I didn't feel the need to because I knew I was never exposed to it. Yet, I couldn't stop worrying about it. So I researched the transmission rates from infected females to males in different modes of sexual contact. I multiplied these probabilities by the number of times I performed that activity with each girl, and then added these figures together for all of the girls I could think of. Each permutation was also multiplied by the national HIV incidence rate for women to account for the chances of each girl actually having HIV. I still remember that the rate of transmission of HIV from an infected female to a male, from unprotected vaginal intercourse, was 1:1000. I don't remember what the final chance of me having contracted HIV was. These calculations were done with all the accuracy and skills I had at that point in time. I did all the formulas and calculations in Excel. I almost wish I still had the spreadsheet. This activity could be interpreted as a sleazy boy counting all of the notches in his belt—glorifying his number of sexual partners. Far from that, it was an obsession that I spent way too much time on, and I wished I never wanted to do it to begin with.

The chances of me contracting HIV wasn't just about the fear of death. It was also the fear of losing future chances for sexual activity. It was about the fear of accidentally infecting someone else. It was the fear of wasting away in a slow death where eventually my body would be unable to fight off a cold. There was a huge fear of vulnerability in that fear. There was a huge fear of losing passion mixed in there. This made a potent concoction of anxiety. This anxiety would never go away, because there was always the chance that I had already been infected but didn't know it. Even if I settled into a monogamous relationship, there was still the chance of one of us contracting it from someone else by cheating. There was no safety. I talked to other boys, and they had similar fears. One friend had a bad case of acid reflux, and he would throw up every morning and at various times during the day. He said he thought he had HIV. He was relieved when the doctor diagnosed him with acid reflux. I'm sure the HIV hype scared a lot of people, but I don't know if anyone was as terrorized as me. A person who never got it, was never exposed to it, and indeed, barely ever heard of anyone who ever contracted it. Of the people I heard contracted it, it was always a friend of a friend of a friend, and they were all career gay men. Now, in the 2020s, HIV medication is advertised on TV the same way that diabetes medicine is. The people who are treated for HIV cannot even detect it in their system. It never became a disease for heterosexual people. It never killed as many people as predicted. The initial emergence of this disease scared so many people who didn't really need to worry about it.

ANXIETY: THE ULTIMATE TRUTH

The deepest source of anxiety is losing oneself, as I stated previously, and the ultimate source is losing oneself totally, which is death. That is the ultimate fear, and it is possible every day, so anxiety is omnipresent. Upon acceptance of death, or losing the fear of it completely, anxiety has the chance to go away. Of course, there are other major fears that could bring about anxiety. One of my major fears is becoming paralyzed or encountering another permanent disability that, in my opinion, limits me from reaching what I want or could have become. I am afraid of becoming less. This is a stupid fear, because I already have a mental illness that some consider a disability. Without this disability, *I never would have become what I became.* So then, disabilities can actually be a benefit, because they open up possibilities for growth that cannot exist without them.

When I was a child, I had to get stitches a few times, but I never got seriously hurt. My body felt very durable, and I wasn't afraid of getting seriously injured. Well, that's not quite true. During the years that I played baseball, I was never as good of a hitter as I could have been if I hadn't always been afraid of getting hit by the pitcher throwing fastballs across the plate. Maybe this was because I understood how easy it was to accidentally hit someone with a pitch, being a baseball pitcher myself at the time.

There was an important caveat regarding death when I was younger. I was raised as a Baptist Christian. Like many Christians, I was taught to believe that the world was wicked, and that the world was going to end during my lifetime. At the end of the world, Jesus would appear in the sky and "rapture" all of the believers into heaven, and they would be spared the tribulations that would be spawned upon those who were left. The Rapture was the event where the believers were teleported into heaven instantaneously. A lot of people still believe this. At the time, my dad believed it, and so did my pastor and the rest of the congregation, so it seemed a solid thing to believe. I had already accepted Jesus Christ as my savior, so I was certainly saved and would be raptured into Heaven. Because of this belief, I very seriously believed that I would be beamed up at rapture time and would never have to die in a conventional way. Looking back, as far as death anxiety is concerned, this rapture belief is a huge benefit.

Many years later, all of my engineering training, secular exposure, and increased quenching of my thirst for knowledge led me to seriously question my religious beliefs. My religious beliefs were still rooted in the fundamental Baptist Christian wheelhouse. I realized that the earth wasn't six thousand years old, that evolution was true, and that there may not be a heaven. What scared me more than hell was nonexistence, a concept I still can't quite grasp. I started searching everywhere I could to find new answers. I read every physics book that attempted to explain the true nature of reality. I read accounts of DNA being linked to cosmic forces. I explored the world's other major religions. I researched spiritualism, mediumship, and ghosts. I studied all of this with a fervor equal to my college studies, both undergraduate and graduate school. When I was a child, my dad said that the studying of these things was linked to Satan's deception of the Word of God, and that they were to be avoided, lest the loss of one's soul. I arrived at the conclusion that consciousness—not just human consciousness—was at the forefront of everything, and that we were living in a sort of dream of cosmic hologram. I knew that everything was unified. This was not as good as being raptured, but it was a conclusion, and a sort of consolation prize. However, I realized, for the first time in my life, around age twenty-eight, that I was definitely going to die someday, just like everyone else.

The irony of the next step can't be understated. It was the year 2009. A year earlier I had gone to a psychologist for some help with depression. She decided to run a battery of tests on me before treating me. Her conclusion was that I was bipolar. My father and sister were also bipolar, but they had literally lost their minds right in front of me. To me, that was a necessary prerequisite to having the condition, not realizing there were multiple forms of it. "I couldn't be bipolar," I said. "I never lost my mind before." I also didn't believe the diagnosis because I didn't want to have a mental illness. So I didn't believe the diagnosis and went on as usual. However, all the spiritual searching I did in 2009 awoke something inside of me. It started happening in earnest as I was finishing reading the book *The New Earth,* by Eckhart Tolle.

I will describe manic experiences in more detail in later chapters. All of my spiritual studies produced an increasing series of resonances the likes of which I had never experienced before. When I was almost finished reading *The New Earth,* a fever pitch of spiritual energy surged throughout my being. It was not only a passive surge, but I learned that by concentrating in indescribable ways that I could control this spiritual energy. I remember, in particular, being able to flow the energy to my hands. This flow expanded outward and it felt like there were two orbs where my hands are.

Next, I became convinced that each person was a representation of one of the characters of the Bible. For instance, 1 percent of people were John the Baptist[15]. I reasoned that the point of life was to find out which character you were, and to act out modern life in a way similar to your respective Bible character. Of course, I came to the conclusion that I was "a Jesus"—as opposed to "the Jesus"—and that my goal was to preach the gospel with my disciples to help change the world to the way it was supposed to be. I didn't think it was blasphemous to consider myself "a Jesus," because I was acknowledging that I wasn't the only one. This distinction made the whole delusion more plausible and, possibly,

---

15 This would correspond to John the Baptist accounting for 1:100 Bible characters, even though this is not true.

less blasphemous. During the course of my "mission," someone called the police, and they took me to the psychiatric hospital.

When I eventually got my mind back in the hospital[16] I was told that I was indeed bipolar, and that I needed psychiatric treatment. I had no counterargument this time. It was clear that I had totally lost my mind, just like my dad and sister before me. I was a little happy to receive the diagnosis, because now I knew there was a problem to be treated, and that that treatment could improve my life. My ex wife didn't share this insight. Her mom was severely bipolar, and she had many memories of her mother and her being tormented by her mother's illness. I remember the look of disappointment and sadness on her face as the psychiatrist explained the diagnosis to us. My smile faded, and I felt like a piece of trash, a misfit rejected from the assembly line of life.

Being diagnosed bipolar really made me feel my mortality. It made me realize that my mind, my most sacred possession, wasn't actually mine, and could be lost like anything else. Losing my mind had terrified me beyond anything that I had ever experienced before.[17] At any second, I felt I could lose my mind. My only prevention was my medication. I started being obsessive about taking it. I would count my pills. I would count them again. And again, and again... Then, when I wasn't around my pillbox, I would try to remember taking my pills, and I would become afraid that I actually had forgotten to take them. This continued and extended into other things. Moles and blemishes on my skin

---

16 Fading back into reality and your normal mind is something that most people can't imagine. It's real. It's also real fighting for your mind back after you get out of the hospital, just like someone trying to lose weight and trying to get back into shape, except harder.

17 If you're feeling bad for me at this moment, don't. This is hard to understand for anyone who hasn't experienced mania several times, but I wouldn't mind getting sick at all right now if not for the disruption to my work and my family. Mania can be very fun, and this is actually an understatement. However, a path of elation can quickly derail into fear and darkness which is very hard to resist.

started to get inspected, lest I had skin cancer. Bumps under my skin, from my lymph nodes, were inspected for symmetry. When symmetry wasn't found, I had to convince myself that the little bumps were just my lymph nodes. I would repeat obsessive phrases to my ex wife, and she would repeat them back to humor me. She scoffed at what was becoming OCD, which was brought on by a bipolar diagnosis. She was getting tired of dealing with it. I could tell. I felt bad. I couldn't help myself though.

So I went back to my psychiatrist, and I told her that the bipolar wasn't really bothering me, but this secondary OCD condition was. She prescribed me medication for it, but it didn't do anything. I actually had a bout of OCD when I was in college, and it was completely vanquished by an antidepressant, but you can't treat Type I bipolar patients with antidepressants, because it triggers mania (it sure does). The OCD continued. My life became hell. My only solace was the oblivion of sleep. During the day, I would just look forward to sleeping. I hated my mind, and how it tormented me.

I got sick again with mania the next year, and then sick again a few months after that, and then I got sick another year after that. Each time I got sick, I didn't mind it as much. The episodes of mania were filled with intense bouts of consciousness with unknown forces, a search for God, and a search for truth. I acknowledged that I was certainly out of my mind during these episodes, but I also knew for sure that there was something real about them. If not real, then something transformative and helpful. My fear of mania diminished, and was replaced by depression that the condition was going to limit what I could do in my life. When I told my doctors and others about the significance and reality of what I was experiencing during mania, they didn't take it seriously, and attributed it to mere neurochemistry gone awry.

I remember thunderous raptures of euphoria and ecstasy, and my entire being orgasming with an electricity that extended by fields beyond my physical body. These climaxes made the happiest happiness I had experienced before almost insignificant. How could a mere imbalance of neurochemistry produce the happiest moments of my life?

After the last time that I got sick, I decided to quit drinking. I had been a solid drinker from age sixteen until I quit at age thirty-one. The doctors kept on telling me I needed to quit because of my illness, and that I would never get better unless I quit. I decided to listen to them to see if they were right. I quit drinking, and I didn't get sick for a long time. During this period of no sickness, I continued to pursue spirituality, chase God, and search for myself. Fortunately, I never found myself.

THERE IS NO ME

I came to the inescapable conclusion that God and I were intertwined as one, as everyone else was, and that *there was no me, andtherefore there was no me to die*. The realization leading up to this and this thought itself were my real rapture. I was taken away by God. There was no me, and I didn't want there to be a me. The symbolic me as I know it will pass, but I won't ever pass. Perhaps I am a Jesus of sort, for:

> *Heaven and earth will pass away, but my words will never pass away. —Matthew 24:35, NIV*

For the first time in years, my OCD and my anxiety melted away. It was like a fog lifting. I was still afraid of the process of dying—who isn't—but the condition of death didn't scare me. I reasoned that I was already dead, before I was born, so it will be just like that after I die. Am I afraid of how it was before I was born? Is anyone afraid of that? Was I afraid of the week-long blackouts during mania?[18] I was conscious, but I had no experience of it. What about when I was a baby or a toddler? Same thing!

If anyone ever wants to escape anxiety, they have to escape the fear of death. It's impossible, you say? It may be the hardest thing you ever do in your life, but it's not impossible. It's worth it. Living without anxiety after living with anxiety is like walking on your feet after walking on your knees.

18 During mania, it is common to black out during the most severe periods of the episode. It is exactly like blacking out when drunk, except it lasts longer. Some blackouts last weeks, and some even months. Unlike a drunk blackout, you tend to rise to full awareness while you're already awake (unlike waking up from a drunken stupor and being conscious). It's like a stone skipping across a lake, the skipping is far apart at first, becomes closer and closer, and finally sinks into the lake.

CHAPTER 6: DON'T BE AFRAID OF LOSING YOUR ANGER

In past chapters, we concluded that anger was the opposite of fear. Of course, to many, the title of this chapter is another paradox. Many people are afraid of *not* being angry, because they think it will make them weak. In my custom of presenting movie quotes, at least some of which I hope you recognize, I will present some now. In the movie *Logan,* a dying Logan says to Laura, a mutant bred to be a killer, "Don't be what they made you." Remembering Chapter 1, this is what I'm saying to you.

HOW ANGER CAN RUN ITS COURSE

Another quote: in *Batman Begins,* Batman's mentor and trainer says to the future Batman, "Your anger gives you great power, but if you let it, it will destroy you." Before anger creates self-destruction, the following may stop it in its tracks:

- Vengeance
    - ◊ This then leads to lack of purpose
    - ◊ Vengeance is often fueled by blind anger that never considers what will happen after it is fulfilled
- Fatigue and Age
    - ◊ Anger dissolves in older men and women. In some crabby few, it remains.
- A realization that it is pushing away loved ones
- Determining that it's a mask for other emotions like:
    - ◊ Self-loathing
    - ◊ Fear
    - ◊ Emotional Confusion
- Attainment of Life Happiness
- Justice
    - ◊ A wrong somewhere has been righted
- Life becomes less complicated and less stressful
- Someone develops a sense of humor, or an even better sense of humor

It's great if any of these things, or something else, naturally causes anger to dissipate. Even if it does, anger may crop up again. It's better to have some tools at your disposal to help your anger ebb away before it destroys you.

ANGER AS A BLOWFISH

Anger is just like a blowfish in action. It's the puffing up of one's mind, body, and mouth n the face of something bigger than you. Because we have minds that can ponder both the past, present, and future, anger triggers do not just exist in the present though. We often think of something in the past, sometimes even what happened earlier that day, and then become angry about it after we conclude that it somehow lessened us. "How dare she say that!" "He was really cruising for a bruising!" Then we let the time machine of our minds venture into the future. We anticipate events that will make us angry even before they happen. "If I catch my daughter trying to wear that risqué outfit, she will really be in for it!" We want to be angry because it makes us feel powerful. We seek out things that anger us to feel this power. Why do we do this?

In Western Society , there are many threats to our ego. Life is very competitive. The day we are born we are measured, and compared to what an average baby should weigh. Babies are scored on the Apgar score. Later, babies are gauged on how well they are following the milestone schedule of sitting up, crawling, and walking. Parents are already worrying if their babies are good enough. This continues to school, to college, to jobs, to partners, and to life in general.

Women are often observed saying, "She thinks she's better than me!" This woman will treat the other woman scornfully from the start. What does a better person look like, compared to a lesser one? Well, a woman thinks that if another woman is prettier than she herself is, she's most likely "better." Or, the prettier woman thinks she's better than the other woman because she knows she's prettier. Here's the funny thing: the prettier woman is probably insecure and may think that the other woman is the prettier one. If a man has a girlfriend, and he sees a taller, more handsome, or rich man around his girlfriend, he may feel insecure. "That man is a better catch. Who would blame her if she left me for her?" he reasons. After the fear and fleeting dejection, the anger arises as a defense mechanism. He may surveil the other man to make sure he's not looking at his girlfriend. If he makes the determination that he is, other angry measures will follow—the ultimate one being fisticuffs.

I grew up in an area where there was a lot of drinking, bars, and bar fights. At that time, bar fighting wasn't really punished by the law to the extent that it is now, or at all, so it was very common. I was told, by a veteran bar patron, "Nine times out of ten, bar fights are over women. Half the time, it's because the women were cheating or dating more than one guy at a time." If a man's ego is hurt by an unfaithful or promiscuous girlfriend, his most primitive and reflexive recourse, especially when drunk, is to assault the other man. This violence builds his ego back up. The thing I never understood was the reasoning for attacking the third party; that person doesn't know you, therefore they really don't owe you anything. Additionally, they may not have been told the truth about your relationship by the person doing the cheating. I have witnessed married women carrying out entirely new relationships while they are still married under quite normal circumstances. What did they tell the new man? They told him that she was still married, but was in the process of separation, residing together, but sleeping in separate rooms. The other man bought that. Would you? He was getting laid by someone new. Why would he care enough to check up on it? It's easier to get angry and attack the third party than deal with the real cause of the hurt—your partner. Sorrow, betrayal, regret, feelings of inadequacy, and uncertainty about the relationship's future are all so complicated compared to anger. However, they will need to be dealt with after the blows settle and the bar stools are righted. The person to be angry at is the cheating partner—not the third party. The third party owes nothing to the person cheated on, unless he or she is bound by morality and knows he is in a love triangle.

With so many triggers, it's easy to get angry. What's worse is that it's empowering and addictive. Why would someone want to give up something like that? Well, for one, it's bad for you. Anger releases stress hormones in the body, increases blood pressure, increases your pulse, and has other negative health implications. Not only that, but anger also leads to social isolation. Nobody wants to be around someone who will blow up at any second over anything. Often, people who have power over and have to interact with subordinates (such as bosses) get spared this because their position cements the interaction; they never realize that anger can lead to loneliness. Indeed, scaring people away and feeling lonely can motivate one to keep one's temper. People are more likely to confide in and tell things to peaceful people than angry people. The peaceful people are levelheaded, offer advice, and listen to the person without getting angry. A traditional example of this is a stay-at-home mom. One of her kids does something very bad. Mother is upset about it, but keeps her head. The kid pleads with their mother, "Please don't tell Dad when he gets home!" This is in anticipation that their father will deal with the situation much more angrily and perhaps violently. Why do the fathers deal with such situations more angrily? It's probably because they have less time at home, and want home to be a peaceful place when they finally arrive there. Generally speaking, fathers tend to have less patience when dealing with children although I have seen stay-at-home-dads with sublime patience. A child misbehaving tarnishes that home time. The quickest way to resolve it is to be angry, as is the case in the face of so many problems.

LAUGHING INSTEAD OF PUNCHING

The best solution to eliminating anger is humor. How many times have you been in a very tense situation, and you were scared of an angry outburst only to be relieved when one person, and then the whole room, erupted in laughter? Did you ever think about why some situations end this way and others do not? There could be one person in the room not taking the situation too seriously. He could have a look on his face that is the catalyst for the humor. Or, it could be one humorous remark. In almost every provoking situation, there is an opportunity to laugh it off.

Let's imagine two people in a physical fight. For those two people, they are experiencing a variety of negative, and even some positive, emotions. They are angry, afraid, unsure of themselves, and completely exhausted. Thirty seconds into a fight and you'll feel like you just ran ten miles. If you've never been in a fight, just trust me on that one. However, the people watching the fight have different emotions entirely. Some people are cheering, even whooping at the fighters. Other people watch with worried faces. And some people are laughing. It is funny when people fight. Why is it funny? Should we feel cruel when we laugh at people fighting? Here is an indirect example of a violent situation being defused, or morphed into entertainment, by humor. Sometimes, when I see my two daughters being catty with each other and fighting, even when they start slapping and kicking each other, my first impulse is to smile. It's funny. Then I put my dad hat on and break it up and discipline them. I have given many serious lectures to my children, and behind my mask of authority, I thought the whole ordeal was funny, and I wanted to laugh. I remember my dad giving me similar lectures, but he was unable to keep his poker face on and he erupted in laughter and immediately ended the lecture.

THE REASON WHY PEOPLE LAUGH IS NOT FUNNY

Humor breaking up anger is a curious situation. I am going to offer an explanation for why this is so. Of course this is only a theory, but it fits the theme of this book, and if you fully believe humor is a solution to anger, you will be more likely to embrace it. I originally encountered this explanation in Robert Heinlein's famous[19] science fiction book, *Stranger in a Strange Land.* At the zoo, observing monkeys, the main character observed a monkey beating a smaller monkey so he could steal his banana. He erupted in laughter. Later, he offered this explanation:

> "I've found out why people laugh. They laugh because it hurts so much . . . because it's the only thing that'll make it stop hurting."

Does that reason sound familiar? It's the same reason people get angry. Remember the three laws of anger. When someone trips and falls, you laugh, unless it's a serious fall. In every comedy movie, the main character is a loser that gets picked on. Remember, *The Waterboy; Hot Rod; Bad Santa; Planes, Trains and Automobiles, and The 40 Year Old Virgin?* Most comedies have a character like the main character in these movies.

If someone is getting picked on, and you're a third-party

19 One of the covers for this book even states "The most famous science fiction book ever written." That's a bold proclamation, but this book's title made it into the lyrics of "We Didn't Start the Fire" by Billy Joel.

observer, you can laugh. You can keep on laughing up to a point. There's a limit. The limit is different for every person and situation, but it's there. If the bully goes too far, and the victim begins to cry, you may stop laughing. You may even tell the bully to back off. The hurt became too much to laugh at, just like someone falling and seriously hurting themselves.

Consider someone having a really, really bad day. Let's say they were stuck in traffic, were late for work, got lectured by their boss, missed work deadlines, had an argument with their ex-spouse, had their electricity turned off because the bill didn't get paid, and had to eat cereal for dinner. Picture the person collapsed against their refrigerator, pondering their day. Instead of feeling sorry for themselves, they being to laugh. They laugh harder and harder. However, soon the laughs start to devolve into sobs, and then the person begins to sob uncontrollably. This is like the third person watching someone getting picked on. The emotion changes from humor to sadness. This was, perhaps, a situation too dire to laugh at.

Is it a coincidence that extreme laughter eventually causes tears, and eventually side-splitting pain? Have you ever laughed so hard, gasping, that you were begging the source of the laughter to stop? It's hard to imagine, but it happens. I have laughed so hard that my ribs were in pain for days. Humor works like this:

Figure 6-1: Humor Instantly Dissolving Anger

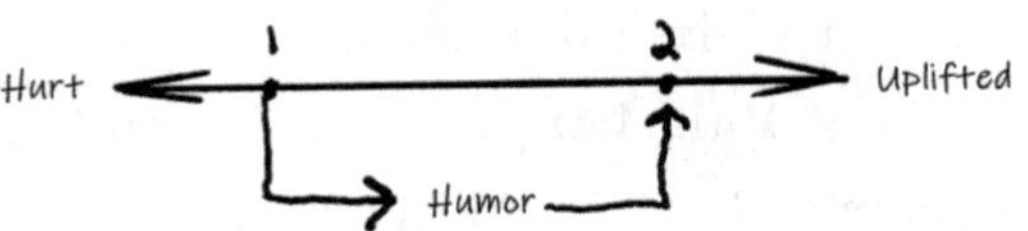

Figure 6-2: Humor Transforming Hurt

So, as already stated, humor dissolves an angry mood or situation, and masks the true nature of a hurtful situation.

LAUGHING AT YOURSELF

One of the hardest things to do is to laugh at yourself, and not take yourself too seriously. "What am I, a joke?" someone would say in response to this. Sure, sometimes you can be a joke. Why not? It's better than being angry. It's more truthful, too. Laughing at yourself is uplifting a hurtful situation to one that doesn't hurt as much.

FEAR'S WEAKNESSES

The secret sauce here is that you don't have to be fearful of losing your anger to fear. Even a fearful situation can be translated into humor. Let's imagine that you're at the gym. Picture that large, muscular man that's at every gym, and he's lifting large weights very angrily and seriously. Let's say he can't complete a lift and starts having a temper tantrum. You could be afraid, watching him. You can be afraid that maybe he'll get mad at you because he's angry already, and that he may do something bad to you. Or, you can look at him and find it funny that he's getting so angry at metal weights. It's like trying to punch a rock. With this thought, you can laugh.

There is this amusement park that I have been going to for over thirty years. It has a very famous haunted house ride. The first time I rode it, at age five, with my aunt, I was so scared I just covered my eyes and ears the entire time. Then, I could ride with my head uncovered and only flinch at the sounds and props even though I was still pretty scared. Later, I would ride fearlessly, even a little bored. As an adult, I would laugh and laugh, and laugh even harder at how scared my children got by the ride. The way my feelings evolved from when I first rode this ride until now, from terror to glee, is an example of how you can do the same thing with your fear. Turning fear into laughter is like the end of a Scooby Doo episode where the monster is unmasked, only to be old Mr. Johnson, trying to scare away the kids from his golf course.

When we get scared, we may default to anger out of self-defense. We fight instead of flight. As we mature, the number of fearful situations decreases. I said I used to be afraid of flying. I now know that flying in a plane is far safer than driving a car. The reason people still fear flying, even in light of that fact, is because of the fatality rate of the plane crashes. I also now know all of the engineering safety factors and strict maintenance protocols that airlines follow. I'm not at all afraid to fly now. I hate flying because it's uncomfortable, but I am not afraid of it. Kids are afraid of thunderstorms. After they mature, and they learn the cause of thunderstorms, their fear goes away. Fearful emotions always carry the burden of the unknown with them. What will happen? Will it hurt me? If it hurts me, how badly will it hurt? Fear goes like this, with knowledge, experience, and predictability:

As Number of Fearful Events ↑ Feelings of Fear ↓

As Knowledge of Fearful Events ↑ Feelings of Fear ↓

As Degree of Unknown ↓ Feelings of Fear ↓

That said, if you're afraid of something, and you'd rather eliminate your fear without using anger, try the following:

- Whatever it is you're afraid of, just do it. After you do it, you'll know more about what it is, what happens after you do it, and it will become more known to you. This is like riding a scary roller coaster the first time. You'll never be as afraid of riding that roller coaster as you were the first time you rode it.
- Research and find out as much as you can about it. People think that we now live in the most dangerous society there ever was—the 2020s. The truth is actually the opposite—it's safer now than it's ever been. National news showcases every murder, burglary, robbery, home invasion, and assault that ever occurs nationwide. This makes these crimes seem commonplace, but the news source is covering three hundred million people when it used to cover less than a million people. So the kids in the 1960s that were allowed to roam around town until the streetlights came on were in more danger than the 2020 kids would be if their parents let them do it.
- Learn to laugh at it. Look at it from a different point of view. It may suddenly become a joke where before it was scary.

A SICK JOKE

One final thought, and this borders on insanity. Consider life for a moment in its entirety. You're born in a completely unknown place that has billions of years of history to catch up on, you're born to random parents and a random family that has many years of history before you, you have no idea how you got here, you have no idea why you're here, you have no idea where you came from, you don't know where you're going, you don't know how much time you have, and you're supposed to figure this all out in a lifetime! Purposely doing this to someone would be a sick joke, and yet this is the situation we all find ourselves in. *Life itself is a sick joke!*

CHAPTER 7: DON'T ENVY ME BECAUSE I'M NOT JEALOUS

Jealousy is a hugely destructive force. Jealousy was defined in Chapter 2. Envy is similar to jealousy, but carries some critical differences. Envy is mere covetousness; it's the wanting of something that someone else has.

The object of envy is normally something that's desirable anyway—its covetousness is just enhanced when someone else wants or has it.. It translates an unthought-of possibility into an actuality. For example, TV and other media are full of billionaires. We hear about them all the time. But we never meet them. Imagine you're at a party and you meet a billionaire or overhear the things that the billionaire is talking about. Suppose he's talking about billionaire things like his yacht, his investments, and his trips around the world. Suddenly, you find yourself envious of the billions of dollars he has. You wish *that you were a billionaire. You envy the billionaire.*

Jealousy, in the sense used in this book, is damage to one's ego in light of favorable circumstances or objects obtained by or bestowed upon another person. Jealousy is so common that I'm surprised no one really stops to think about how damaging it is. Womenperhaps as a result of still being in a more passive position in society[20] than men, are very prone to jealousy, because they are expected to be passive and to receive compliments and gifts from others. This is passive positive reinforcement. On Valentine's Day, or anniversaries, traditionally, the husband or boyfriend will give special gifts or pay for special dates to mark the occasion. Men, on the other hand, get praise and adulation by more active means. Men are more prone to envy than women, because they wish they could have obtained, or done, what another obtained or has by active means. "I wish I had become a professional baseball player," they say, after envying the baseball players on TV. This is a mild case of envy. A common form of envy in men is coveting another man's wife or girlfriend. This is envy of a dangerous sort; this type of envy has resulted in much suffering, pain, and premature death.

Women are most jealous of each other. The thing they are most jealous of are things that attract the feelings, desire, attention, and money of men. This would suggest that the ultimate goal of women is to attract desirable men and experience romantic love. This is supported by the huge sales of romance novels, which are bought mostly by women. An episode of *Grey's Anatomy*

---

20 Despite the 20th Century liberation of women, their equal presence in the work force, and how they are now better educated than their male counterparts, executive roles, positions of power, and earnings are still dominated by men. Because of this, I would say that they still occupy a passive position in society. They also tend to take less risks than men and are not rewarded for assertive behavior. Assertive female bosses, for example, are often not seen as just assertive.

is gray because it's more about the anatomy explored during passion, and not medicine.

Women know that men very much care about how a woman looks. Therefore, they become very jealous of beautiful women. The more beautiful, the more the jealousy. Surprisingly, women are also jealous of the attention that other women receive from each other. Indeed, women evaluate and critique each other's looks to a much further extent and in more detail than men do. Sometimes, they do this overtly, but they more often do this in secret. A man sees a woman, rates her as a one to a ten, and then ogles her for a time proportionate to her score[21]. The currency of women is attention. The jealousy equation can be simplified to:

(Extent of Jealousy) = MF (Attention Others Receive – Attention Received) + FF* (Attention Others Receive – Attention Received)*

Where

MF = weighting factor of the attention of men

FF = weighting factor of the attention of women

Different people assign different factors to MF and FF in their heads, so they cannot be defined here.

It's no secret that women like or love men with money. Why wouldn't they? Even in simple hunter gatherer societies, the man who could provide the most food and shelter was highly desirable. That said, in modern society, a woman's lifestyle, the type of home she lives in, the clothes she wears, and gadgets she will have access to is directly dependent upon the earnings of her

21 A very beautiful woman is referred to as "a knockout." This is stating that she is a 10, because a 10 count is necessary to declare a knockout in boxing. I used to think it was because she was so beautiful it would figuratively knock you out, but, looking back on that, it doesn't make sense.

man (or woman). Of course, women can make their own money, but they still don't earn as much money as men,and men don't use a woman's finances as dating criteria. Besides the lifestyle benefits, time is money, and money is crystalized time. When a man spends money on a woman, he is actually spending time on her, spending attention on her. Even the DeBeers diamond convention of "two months' salary" as the amount to be spent for an engagement ring is keeping the money-to-crystalized-time conversion in mind.

The reason why jealousy is so dangerous is that it can prompt someone to damage the other person to even the score. In other words, they take down the other person to compensate for the damage the jealousy caused to them. It's vengeance when no wrong was committed. It's like sentencing an innocent woman to prison. A girl can be jealous that another girl has a handsome boyfriend. She is both envious and jealous. Therefore, she tries to take the boyfriend from the girl. This scenario plays out in bars all the time. Single women are more likely to sleep with a married man than a single man—at least for one-night stands. This feat does two things. It makes the woman feel like she's triumphed over the ghost wife by taking her man from her for one night. It's also because the man is married and there will be no future involvement with the taker. Another scenario is someone observes that someone has a nice car. This someone decides to key the car. This will cause duress to the car's owner, and he will certainly not like his car as much until he gets it fixed.

To triumph over greed, we must realize that jealousy is only greed in disguise. Jealousy is the belief that "Everything good should come to me, and if it comes to someone else, I either feel negative towards them or towards myself." Jealousy is for people who fail to be happy for other people when they experience something positive in their lives. There are some feigned congratulatory gestures and praise, but they aren't genuine. Everyone knows the difference between pretending to be happy for someone and actually being happy for them. However, some people have yet to feel what it feels like to actually be happy for someone when they have something good happen to them. This sounds strange, but it's true.

Kids are honest about jealousy. I have seen good birthdays for kids result in other kids crying in their rooms out of jealousy. "Don't worry, sweetie, it will be like this for you when your birthday comes." Some parents anticipate so much jealousy from their other kids that they buy consolation gifts for them so they don't feel too left out. In one particular instance, I planned a surprise birthday celebration for my wife. It wasn't anything huge, but a lot of effort went into it. This resulted in my son, who was about eight at the time, crying in his room because he was jealous of his mom's birthday. I'd like to say that I dealt with that situation with grace and wisdom, but I met it with with a deal of anger and lecturing.

Jealousy will never be vanquished without halting greed. Our society is greedy and materialistic. It's no surprise that some people are greedy. "I'm not greedy," they say, "I don't love money." Those are the same people who always ask to split the bill when out with friends, or let others cover the tab and never offer to pay the tab themselves. They're also the people who spend all their disposable income on the latest iPhone, gadget, or doodad. They can barely pay their rent, but they will spend what they can to satisfy their desire for more. Greed is the pursuit of getting as much as possible for yourself, despite the costs to others or the needs of others.

Greedy people are digging for gold to fill the hole in their hearts. No amount of gold will fill that hole. Conquering greed goes much further than what we have discussed previously. It involves the loss of self, ego death, and how we look at what we are. Even an enlightened person may do something that appears greedy.

I remember dining out while running other errands, and the thought occurred to me, *I feel like buying something.* Actually, it was more like, *I feel like getting something.* It was like being a kid in a candy or toy store. The problem was I didn't need anything. I had everything I needed. The worse problem was that I didn't want anything. I had everything I could possibly want. No, really, I did. Even the big things that people want, I had. I had a nice truck, a great house, a cool dog, a loving family, and a host of gadgets and doodads. Then I realized what I really wanted. *I wanted to want something, and then I wanted to get it.* I wanted anticipation and satisfaction. But, I didn't want anything. So, I decided to go to a store that could potentially entice me with something. Everything looked like stupid trinkets to me, so I left. I was trying to create a void so I could fill it. I wanted to create a problem that didn't exist. Who purposely wants to feel greedy? I'm normally pretty satisfied, so I guess I was greedy in that I wanted to feel greedy. Actually, I know what I wanted: *I wanted a surprise, and it was impossible to give myself one.* I wanted someone to give me something that I wanted that I hadn't thought of beforehand.

Christmas morning can spark scenes of greed. We've all seen it. The kid who opens up presents, and doesn't appreciate any of them. Or the child who, after opening all his presents, laments the ones he didn't get. I remember an interesting scene during my family Christmases. My dad would open up his presents, and sneer, "I'm opening up a present that I bought with my own money." He said it in jest nearly every year, and no one would reply. If I could go back in time now, I would retort with "Yeah, but you can't buy the surprise!"

When I open up Christmas gifts now, I feel that anticipation of surprise, even though I have everything I want. Someone thought up something they thought I would want that I could not think of, or did not want to think of, myself. I don't care if it's a five-dollar gift, but I think I enjoy opening up Christmas gifts now more than when I was a kid. It's because I don't want anything, so there's no chance to lose. As a kid, Christmas was always filled with huge amounts of anticipation, but there were concrete expectations, doubts, a lot of fear, and a lot of excitement. But, very purely, opening up gifts now underscores the cliché "It's the thought that counts." It really is. That's the best gift one can receive from others.

Ultimately, one who has everything they want or need will eventually want a surprise. They will want something that's not under their control, that they can't anticipate. In life, normally when we talk about surprises, it's in a negative sense. Indeed, that's because, as in other contexts, negative things are more heavily weighted than positive ones. When someone reaches the point where they don't really weigh negative things more heavily than positive ones, and learn to accept reality the way it is—unpredictable, ever-changing, easy, hard, a learning experience, setbacks, gains, and everything else—everything will come as a surprise, and a pleasant one at that.

It's like me opening up my gifts now. It may be something I want. It may be something I don't want or don't like, but it will be something that I didn't expect. It will be something that someone else thought I might like. This couldn't happen without the element of not knowing. The unknown is scary, but it's also what brings meaning to our lives.

Someone or something weaved this universe together as a surprise for someone. It was a surprise for you, and a surprise is the gift for the "one who has everything and is impossible to buy for." Surprise yourself, and see if you can only be greedy for surprises. Your greed will always be satisfied, because surprises come every day. The fear of the unknown becomes the anticipation of the unknown. The fulfillment of that unknown is always a surprise.

Surprise yourself by eliminating your greed. Once greed falls, its deadly sister, jealousy, will fall with it. Never again will you scoff and hate yourself at someone else's fortune. Never again will the innocent girl be punished out of another's jealousy. It's justice that's emotional; it's emotional justice.

Emotional Justice = Unburdened Feelings + Acceptance + Anticipation of the Unknown (Surprise)

CHAPTER 8: R-E-S-P-E-C-T

The title of this chapter, which is supposed to be spelled out, as someone in a spelling bee, is reminiscent of the song by Aretha Franklin. I'm sure you have heard the song, but here are the lyrics:

What you want
Baby, I got it
What you need
Do you know I got it?
All I'm askin'
Is for a little respect when you get home (just a little bit)
Hey baby (just a little bit) when you get home
(Just a little bit) mister (just a little bit)

I ain't gonna do you wrong while you're gone
Ain't gonna do you wrong 'cause I don't wanna
All I'm askin'
Is for a little respect when you come home (just a little bit)
Baby (just a little bit) when you get home (just a little bit)
Yeah (just a little bit)

I'm about to give you all of my money
And all I'm askin' in return, honey
Is to give me my propers

When you get home (just a, just a, just a, just a)
Yeah, baby (just a, just a, just a, just a)
When you get home (just a little bit)
Yeah (just a little bit)

Ooh, your kisses
Sweeter than honey
And guess what?
So is my money
All I want you to do for me
Is give it to me when you get home (re, re, re, re)
Yeah baby (re, re, re, re)
Whip it to me (respect, just a little bit)
When you get home, now (just a little bit)

R-E-S-P-E-C-T
Find out what it means to me
R-E-S-P-E-C-T
Take care, TCB
Oh (sock it to me, sock it to me, sock it to me, sock it to me)
A little respect (sock it to me, sock it to me, sock it to me, sock it to me)
Whoa, babe (just a little bit)
A little respect (just a little bit)
I get tired (just a little bit)
Keep on tryin' (just a little bit)
You're runnin' out of fools (just a little bit)
And I ain't lyin' (just a little bit)
(Re, re, re, re) when you come home
(Re, re, re, re) 'spect
Or you might walk in (respect, just a little bit)
And find out I'm gone (just a little bit)

This song was originally released by Otis Redding in 1965. Franklin's version came out in 1967 and turned out to be the hit. R E S P E C T was sung in an era where women were often treated poorly by their spouses. In her song, she is assuring she will do everything in her power to treat her man right, even giving him all her money, and all she is asking for in return is "just a little bit" of respect. What's more, she's asking for it nicely.

Respect was precisely defined in Chapter 2. Showing respect

for someone, even just a little, is another form of manners that carefully glues society together. If you can't respect someone as a person, you can at least respect their opinions, values, religion, beliefs, and their basic rights as a human being. Rights aren't bestowed upon people by the universe, but by the laws and standards of society.

It's interesting to note one area where respect is extremely important—about as important as money is in normal society. In prison, everything is about respect. I am referring to male inmates here. Based upon the numerous prison documentaries I have watched, I don't think respect is nearly as important in female facilities. Respect from other inmates, and even the guards, is about the only valuable thing prison inmates have left. As an inmate forms a reputation in prison, the respect he receives from others either increases or decreases. Unfortunately, violent behavior that breaks the rules of prison and the laws that still apply in prison (like laws prohibiting severe assault and murder) results in increased respect for inmates. As I said, fear of a person is often a prerequisite for respect. Indeed, prison inmates test new inmates by fighting them to see how well they can fight back and if it is possible to fear, and, consequently, respect them. The Convict Code, the informal rules of conduct for inmates, is based on a hierarchy of respect. Even criminals, outside of prison, strongly value respect from other criminals and people within their syndicates.

If someone respects you, it's essentially a shield to your ego. It's a guarantee that they won't damage your ego or hurt your feelings without a strong reason for doing so. When someone respects us, we feel comfortable around them. The greatest degree of comfort is achieved when a mutual respect is attained. Respect is similar to trust, but without full control or power entrusted to the respected person. Respect also does not require any affinity towards the respected person. Trust is normally associated with love or endearment.

Respect = Trust – Abdicated Control – Affinity

Respect also shows empathy. We know that we feel a deep desire to feel respected, so we want to bestow that respect upon someone else as well. The tricky thing about respect is that it has to be earned. It is earned when a person observes someone performing or doing something that they find skillful, admirable, difficult, or morally acceptable. Respect has a gauge, or an allotted amount for each person. This gauge is dynamic, and measures respect in the same way that a thermometer measures temperature, except it has a memory component to it. More than that, respect tends to have a default gauge for people in certain positions, jobs, or who have had such positions or performed some service. For example, veterans are respected by most people, because they risked their lives to serve their country. They risked their lives to save people they didn't know personally. Similarly, fire fighters are respected because they risk their lives in order to save people they also do not know. However, default respect, based upon past or present position, isn't the same for everyone. People with a criminal history, for example, would tend to respect police offers less than the average law-abiding citizen. There are rankings of prestige (similar to respect) of professions. Here is the list, from top to bottom:[22]

22 https://en.wikipedia.org/wiki/Occupational_prestige#List_of_occupations_by_prestige

Prestige scores

Occupation	Prestige
Physicians	86.05
Lawyer	74.77
Computer systems analyst or scientist	73.70
Teacher	73.51
Physicist or astronomer	73.48
Chemist	73.33
Architects	73.15
Biological or life scientist	73.14
Physical scientist, not elsewhere classified	73.09
Chemical engineer	72.30
Professor	71.79
Judge	71.49
Engineer (not elsewhere classified)	70.69
Chief executive or general administrator, public administration	70.45
Geologist or geodesist	69.75
Psychologist	69.39
Manager, medicine and health	69.22
Aerospace engineer	69.22
Clergy	68.96
Civil engineer	68.81

This list is based on occupations in the US. The perception in other countries is very different, and this list would appear differently per each country. Physicians are at the top of the list because people interface with them often, and they are trusted to maintain or increase someone else's health, or even save their life. Doctors have someone's life at their fingertips. Lawyers also top the list because their services and skill have direct and lasting impact on someone's life. A defense lawyer can stop someone from getting sent to jail for the rest of their life. A civil lawyer might obtain millions of dollars by suing another entity. People are also familiar with lawyers, and most people have had to retain one at least once in their lives. Engineering is a very poorly understood profession. Because of this, engineering is often referred to as "the stealth profession." A multitude of things that touch every aspect of our society were created by engineers—almost every technological device, machine, developed piece of land, and things that touch every aspect of our society were created by engineers. The moon landing, the greatest technological achievement in the history of mankind, was made possible by engineers—not scientists. Because the finished products are taken for granted, the engineers unseen, and the skill needed to perform engineering is unknown, engineers are not respected as much as doctors or lawyers. It is interesting to note that engineers command the highest level of prestige in certain countries. This prestige extends so far that engineers are introduced as "Engineer Paul," in the same way that doctors are introduced as "Dr. Smith," even when they are outside of the hospital. I am an engineer, so of course I am sympathetic of the lack of prestige that engineers command in American.

The point is that someone's default level of respect is based on a combination of things: their occupation, their socioeconomic status, their physical appearance, their relationship to the other person, and their height and weight. Tall people command a higher level of respect, even though this really has nothing to do with how much respect they should command. Really beautiful people, while sought after, may actually command less respect because it is assumed they aren't very intelligent. Figure 8-1 below illustrates how different elements of respect may come together to form an aggregate level of respect.

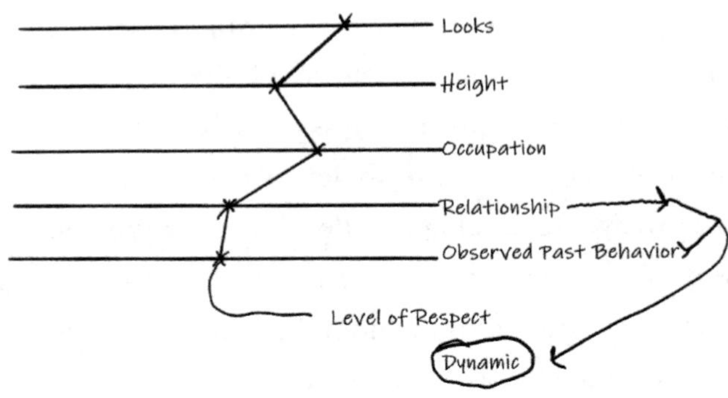

Figure 8-1: Aggregate Respect Diagram

Just like in prison, the observed past behavior changes as people interact with each other. This observed behavior can initiate, increase, decrease, or even destroy any level of respect. Similarly, the relationship between two people, which can also evolve, determines the level of respect. A boss is respected to a certain degree because she is the boss. A husband is respected a certain amount, even if unwise behavior is observed for a while. When two people get married, an increase in respect is normally expected. "I'm your wife; you shouldn't treat me that way!" Would she have said that when she was just a fiancé or a girlfriend? I don't know.

So why are we here talking about respect in such detail? The amount someone is respected by other people is almost always proportional to their level of *self-respect*, and their self-respect is related to their ego. Your ego is related to your self-acceptance or how you feel about or love yourself. Self-respect determines how people feel about what is said to them and about them, how they react to certain situations, and when and how they might stand up for themselves. It determines how much a child will tolerate bullying. It dictates if a teenager might cut themselves to evoke a catharsis. The reasons why we respect others echoes in how we respect ourselves. If we respect criminals, we will respect ourselves more if we become criminals, and we are then more likely to become criminals. People gravitate towards both short and long term goals that generate respect. Normally, it's for the respect of others, but sometimes it's directly for self-respect.

So be careful about why you admire or respect someone. Eventually, that same lens will be focused on the mirror, and the same evaluations will be applied to yourself. I just wrote admire AND respect. Why were these two words just used together? How does admiration relate to respect? Admiration merely means you approve or take pleasure in a thing, or a person, or something that person did. It doesn't necessarily impact your future behavior towards a person, if the source of admiration is a person. This is a critical distinction, because respect dictates future behavior and assessments of self and others, while admiration does not. You can admire a singer because she sounds beautiful, but that may not be enough to generate respect for her. Typically, to respect someone you actually have to encounter or know them. You can admire someone from a distance, virtually or physically. There's even the often used phrase "you have a secret admirer." People like to admire anonymously. Admiration is safe. Sometimes people even hide the objects of their admiration. There are hidden magazines, hidden music, and secret crushes. Admiration gives pleasure; respect does not. Admiration is reactive and passive; respect is active after observation or interaction. Respect is a duty or obligation, because it was earned by someone else. It's a repayment. Admiration may lead to imitation in an effort to effect boosts to one's own self-esteem and to recreate the original pleasure of the initial admiration. Here are some contrasting statements about admiration and respect:

- Respect takes effort while admiration is effortless
- Admiration brings pleasure passively while respect takes effort
- Respect tends to be reciprocated; admiration does not
- Respect hones self-respect; admiration can result in imitation
- Admiration may result in a decrease of respect (seeing someone who is very good looking)
- Self-respect is possible; self-admiration is called pride

Passive Observation→Pleasure or Like→Admiration→Copying→False Pride

Observation and Positive Assessment→Similarity to Current or Future Self→Respect→Respect/Disrespect Self for Same Qualities→Self-Respect/Self-Loathing

Make sure you give others respect, when respect is due, but make sure you are respecting people for the right reasons, for you may become like the others you respect. Admiration is normally harmless. But, when admirable qualities are merely copied, admiration rarely leads to pride. A person may feel like a fraud at worst or a hack at best. Self-respect and pride are necessary for good self-esteem, good self-worth, and, later, transcendence above ego.

CHAPTER 9: THINKING IS THE HARDEST WORK THERE IS

There is a famous quote by Henry Ford, which says: Thinking is the hardest work there is, which is probably why so few engage in it.

Daniel Kahneman, a Nobel Prize Laureate, categorized thinking into two categories in his book *Thinking, Fast and Slow.* The hard-work thinking is the slow kind, which takes unfamiliar concepts, situations, places, and the like, and sort of rotates them in the mind for careful analysis. An object that repeatedly undergoes slow thinking eventually gets placed into fast thinking. Fast thinking is intuitive, quick, almost automatic thinking that we apply in situations that we are familiar with, have a lower degree of importance, or that we have thought about or mastered before. People like the fast thinking because it is nearly effortless, and normally involves familiar situations. On the other hand, people avoid slow thinking like the plague, because indeed, it requires a great deal of effort, and probably, as Henry Ford stated, is the hardest work there is.

Albert Einstein said, "We cannot solve our problems with the same thinking we used when we created them." This is another way of saying, "the definition of insanity is doing the same thing over and over again and expecting different results," which is also credited to Einstein. Einstein knew a lot about thinking. His famous theory of relativity is often credited as the greatest scientific breakthrough ever accomplished by a person working mostly alone. According to Einstein himself, who stated he almost had a nervous breakdown while discovering relativity and other physicists, it is also known as one of the single greatest efforts of thinking ever. In order to develop this theory, he had to think completely differently about how we view space and time. His thinking differently is what allowed his scientific breakthroughs.

If we want to better ourselves, solve our problems, we have to think completely differently about how we view ourselves, the world, our past, our future, our regrets, forgiveness, healing, therapy, and achieving wellness. On a quest to wellness, how do you know that you have achieved it? Well, as there is no ultimate degree to how bad a situation can be or how bad off someone can be, so it is with the degree of wellness a person can achieve. It's limitless. You could possess a completely healthy mind and body, but feel your life is lacking because you have no spirituality. You could lack a sense of connectedness to something greater. Intrinsic to the human spirit is a desire to be part of something greater and to seek out a universal force in the universe.

Most people don't want to think. It's too hard. Let's take church, for example. The minister chooses a few Bible verses and creates a one-hour sermon about them. The congregation listens to the few verses and carries home with them the message of the sermon. How many people actually pick up the Bible and read it themselves, and come to their own conclusions? Very few do this. This is because reading the Bible is exceptionally hard. It's something you typically either go through the motions of, with little to no understanding, or pore over meticulously and think about hard as you do it, to generate meaning. In the former case, you do it merely to say you did it, and in the latter you actually get some value out of it (hopefully). At various times in my life, I picked up a Bible and started reading it. Even as a child, I did this. I went through the motions of reading it to make myself feel better, but I did not understand much of what I read. I returned to it, years later, and the same thing happened. Finally, in my later years, I understood what I was reading. Even then, the reading was about as slow as reading a scientific textbook. Reading the Bible takes a great deal of mental effort, and it's something I only do in small pieces when I am rested and have a good deal of mental energy.

What is mental energy? Why can you be stationary all day, doing some heavy mental lifting, and be completely exhausted by the end of the day even though you haven't lifted a finger to do any physical work? It's very possible that nothing outside of your mind changed as a result of your thinking. Unless the extra power output of your brain can be measured compared to a baseline, you haven't done any work in the classical physics definition of it. The firing of all of those neurons and the transmittal of all of those neurotransmitters creates some type of fatigue. There are residual neurotransmitters lying around, and probably some proteins or neuronal material floating around, from the chaos of hard thinking. These thinking remnants may make it more difficult to transmit accurate messages within the brain, and this may be the source of the fatigue. There is probably extra electrical firing within the brain that occurs during heavy thinking. You can drink coffee or some other stimulant to keep going, but the quality of the thinking degrades and is eventually ineffective. The only thing that can restore the mind is sleep. Recent breakthroughs in brain imaging have found that, during parts of sleep, your brain cells actually contract, and the brain is flooded with cerebral spinal fluid that flushes out the residual brain waste described above. Also, mysteriously, the brain must enter the REM stage of sleep, which is when we most dream, to feel rested. A number of studies have concluded that even an adequate amount of sleep, without REM sleep, does not restore a person the way normal sleep, with REM, does. As an example of this without referring to a study, heavy marijuana users experience diminished REM sleep from the active effects of THC on the brain. Eventually, they do not feel rested after sleeping, and report no dreaming at all during sleep.[23]

Let's talk about sleep for a second. I will share with you something that we don't want to hear, because, in our fast-paced world, people pride themselves on how little they sleep. Lack of sleep is associated with a multitude of health ailments, even weight gain, a decrease in cardiovascular health, poor cognition, diabetes, and several others. These days, people have trouble sleeping for a variety of reasons, including stress, busy schedules, artificial lighting, rampant entertainment, and the desire to be more productive. Americans currently average about 6.8 hours of sleep per night. That's the average, so there are many people who sleep less than that. Here's an interesting fact: in the year 1900, the average amount of sleep per person was nine hours. I can surmise this was primarily because there was no artificial

23 From personal conversations with people who report to be heavy marijuana users.

lighting, no nightly entertainment, lives were less stressful, and the expectation of being ultra-productive was lower.

Here's another fact: people with mentally challenging jobs that involve deep thinking, like mathematicians and engineers, need more sleep than people who perform jobs involving heavy physical labor. This makes sense considering the brain repair that has to happen, as described above. People who mentally strain all day, or are under constant mental stress because of anxiety or some other negative mental condition, have to sleep about an hour more than people who only perform physical labor all day with little mental or emotional stress. Most people in the 1900s did not have mental jobs and their lives were less stressful. Therefore, I contend that a person with a mentally taxing job or a great deal of worry should probably get between nine and ten hours of sleep a night. A person with a physical job and a quiet mental disposition should probably get nine hours of sleep a night. This is different than the currently recommended seven to eight hours a night. In fact, it's a full two hours more, which is a lot.

I recently became self-employed, which meant that my alarm clock went through the window. I started waking up whenever I woke up, and I started going to sleep when I was tired. The amount I slept went up to between nine and ten hours a night. At first, I felt ashamed, because of all the highly successful people who brag about accomplishing what they do on four hours of sleep or less. For years before my self-employment, I had traditional day shift jobs where I would have to be at my desk by eight a.m. With the commute, and my wake-up routine, I would get up around six a.m. or earlier. At nighttime, I would rarely go to bed or be able to fall asleep early enough to achieve eight hours of sleep. I would normally fall asleep at eleven and, at best, I would get seven hours of sleep. There were worse days during the week where I would only get six hours of sleep. I was constantly tired, and I compensated for this by drinking copious amounts of coffee and sometimes energy drinks. When I came home at night, after the rush hour commute, I had no energy left to do anything. It was a Herculean effort even to eat (let alone cook) dinner. During my evenings, I would pretty much vegetate on the couch watching TV until bedtime. Sometimes, I would muster up enough energy to go for a walk. I didn't have enough energy to exercise or really do anything else. By Friday, the cumulative effects of this routine would have built up, and I would often take a nap when I got home. The nap would make me feel better, but I was still drained. The only replenishment came from catching up on sleep during the weekends. I would normally sleep between ten and twelve hours on Friday and Saturday night. In my earlier years, my drinking years, this sleep was tainted by drunkenness the night before. Drunkenness deteriorates the quality and positive effects of one's sleep.

When I started to get my nine and a half hours of sleep each night, my life and my being improved dramatically. It was the first time, probably since childhood, that I hadn't felt tired at all. Tasks and obligations felt effortless. My mind was sharper and I could perform my work with relative ease. My endurance increased. After a day of work, I felt like going to the gym or actually doing something. It wasn't only that I *could* go to the gym or do something, *I actually wanted to*, after sitting at a desk all day. I played with the kids more. My energy lasted into nighttime. It wasn't perfect. I still drank a lot of coffee. Because of that, I had caffeine energy spikes and lows, but they weren't that bad, and my energy really wasn't dependent upon coffee (although waking up certainly was). Initially, I thought I was sleeping too much, and that what I was doing wasn't healthy. That was before I encountered the research I presented above whereby I discovered I was doing what everyone should be doing. If you don't believe it, try it. Try sleeping for at least nine hours a night and see how you feel. At the very least, you will want to do the hard thinking that this book is proposing.

There are many other ways to enhance your mental performance. These will be discussed later, but are listed here as:

- A healthy diet
- Intense exercise
- Meditation and other spiritual practices
- Mindfulness
- Deep breathing
- Being consistently engaged in mentally stimulating activities
- Being committed to being a lifetime learner

Once your mind is strengthened by acquiring more endurance, more focus, and less inertia (the tendency to want to stay in its default or current state), it is time to mentally grapple with someone. Who will you be grappling with? You will be grappling with yourself, your mental shadow, the mental boogeyman who has been plaguing you. This is the voice telling you that you can't change your life for the better, that things will never change, that you're a loser. The problem is that you want your life to get better but you don't know how. You may have tried certain things before to this end, but, after they did not work, you became frustrated and hopeless and accepted that things will never get better. Your mental jab will be asking the voice why. "Why can't I do it?" The mental shadow always has quick replies—"Because you've always failed before." If you're learning something new, you will retort, "That's only because I've never tried new things." "You're afraid to try new things," he says. This is a juncture for the mental grappling. This is where you pause the thinking and decide what you need to change. You need to decide what new thing you have to do to overcome the obstacle.

What new thing do you try? There's no wrong answer, because anything new is more likely to work than something you have already done. But, using your mind, you can analyze your problem, what you have done before to try to overcome it, and the available things you have yet to do to try to fight it. You may already have queued up things to do but haven't tried them. This is the easiest place to start. What if it fails? It may fail, but it has a higher chance of working than anything that you've tried before that has already failed. If it fails, you will still learn from the experience. Armed with this new knowledge, you may know what went wrong, why it went wrong, and what to change or what new thing to try next. People say, "Failure is not an option." Failure is within the eye of the beholder. When Thomas Edison tried a thousand materials to serve as a filament for the lightbulb, we can look at that as "he failed a thousand times to find the right filament," or we can just as easily and more optimistically say "he confirmed that a thousand different materials were not suitable filaments." In failing, we still achieve something. We learn, we get new experience, and this experience directs us to a solution. No one was ever the best at something the first time they tried it. When Muhammad Ali put on boxing gloves for the first time, he did not become an instant champion. So it is with this process. There is a quote: "Experience is what you get when you didn't get what you wanted. And experience is often the most valuable thing you have to offer."[24]

After your first failure, the voice comes back and says, "See, you tried something new and you failed just like you thought you would." You, becoming wiser, brush off this remark and say something like, "It didn't completely fail. It worked partially. It only didn't work because..." Let's say the thing you were trying to do was quit smoking. The different way you tried to quit that you had never tried before was "cold turkey." Within a week into your quitting program, you got a phone call that your mother was ill. This caused that deep sinking feeling you get in your gut, that acute anxiety. You naturally craved cigarettes in response to this and caved. So, you say to the voice, "It only failed because I became anxious when I found out my mom was sick." You decide to quit via cold turkey again. This time, you anticipate that something will come about that will rack your nerves. You have an alternative for the cigarettes, which you planned in advance. As life does, within one month into your smoking cessation program, you have an awful fight with your boyfriend. He's threatening to break up with you. A craving for a cigarette explodes within you. Your skin is on fire for a cigarette. You feel it all over. During your cessation program, you have learned to take brisk walks outside, and sometimes jogging for health and stress reduction, and you found that the jogging lessened your smoking cravings. You may have learned these coping skills by trial and error or from advice given by others. You immediately put your walking gear on and take a brisk walk. You begin to jog. You get more bold and break into a run. You think about your fight and run harder, and harder. Something washes over you and the craving for the cigarette

---

24 Randy Pausch, https://www.goodreads.com/quotes/48126-experience-is-what-you-get-when-you-didn-t-get-what

is waning. You realize that there are alternatives to smoking for handling your anxiety. This is a triumphant victory. You begin to believe that you can quit smoking. This situation may repeat itself. The next time, there could be another coping mechanism in place that helps you stave off acute cigarette cravings. Your mind has done all of this since it has become more creative when it comes to solving problems because it is unafraid of looking at them in a different way. It has the energy and willpower to do these new things. You smack the shadow voice with an uppercut and he reels back into the ring. Shadowman can't defend against your new techniques, because he's only ever fought the old you.

It's six months later. You have kept yourself cigarette free. It's been a huge victory, although you're still on the lookout for smoking triggers. On the other hand, the lack of cigarettes has caused an increase in your appetite, you have turned to food for comfort, and consequently have gained twenty pounds. You feel healthier, but every time you look into the mirror or can't fit into your old clothes, you feel a tinge of sadness and a hint of regret for quitting smoking. This is something I can't emphasize enough: *In the process of improving yourself, unintended consequences will arise and you may have new problems to deal with. You can either revert back to how you were or you can face these problems straight on.*

The shadow jumps back into the ring, reinvigorated. "Now you're fat because you quit smoking. You can't do anything right. You just traded one bad thing for another." Your mind races but you quickly retort, "Even though I'm twenty pounds heavier, I'm still healthier than I was twenty pounds ago with cigarettes. Besides, this is a common side effect of quitting smoking, and I can handle it. I'll either deal with the extra weight or I will lose it." At this point, you accept either alternative, but not going back to smoking. This is a huge realization. This is insurance that you won't revert becoming a smoker again. Whether you accept the weight or try to lose it, you've still beaten the cigarettes. *You have nothing to lose but possibly the weight.*

You wonder how you can lose weight. During the course of quitting smoking, you started some light exercising for stress reduction, but you also noticed that your cardiovascular endurance improved. Using this extra wind, you decide you can start your walks with jogs and end them in runs. You begin a jogging program. You end up losing ten pounds, but no matter how hard you try, you can't get that extra ten pounds back off. Your mind kicks in. It needs more data. You start to watch documentaries about health, diet, and weight loss. Several programs mention that, in order to lose weight, it's more important to change your diet first, and then embark on an exercise program. This is because the better nutrition jump starts your metabolism and gives your body a platform for losing fat. You take this advice. It works. You not only lose the remaining ten pounds, but you also lose an extra five pounds, even with some lean muscle added. Your pants size has gone down two sizes. The smoking cessation program built some momentum that led to exercise, better diet, and physical fitness.

You're back in the ring with the shadow again. You counter with two jabs, a hook, and then a massive uppercut, and he falls to the floor. He slowly gets up and rears his ugly shadow face. He sneers, "No matter what you do, you'll…" You immediately counter with a flurry of punches, and end up with a knockout punch. You finish his sentence, "No matter what I want to do, I'll find a way to do it. If I ever find myself in a bad place, I will find a solution out of it." Is that true? You doubt yourself. A million situations start to spin around you, like so many spiderwebs in a suddenly dark place.

- What if I get fired from my job and I get evicted from my apartment?
    - ◊ I'll find another job before losing my home.
    - ◊ I will move in temporarily with friends and family who would be glad to have me. My ego would be bruised, but I would recover from it.
- What if my boyfriend and I break up and I'm alone forever?
    - ◊ He's just one person. Just because he and I don't work out, doesn't mean love won't work out for me.
    - ◊ I will use the experience of being with him to learn what to look for in another partner down the line.
- What if someone I care about dies?
    - ◊ I will grieve for them, as they deserve, I will miss them, but I will get over it.
- What if...
    - ◊ This too shall pass

The boxing ring of your mind is where the solution to all problems begins. Problems aren't just solved, they are fought out until viable solutions are produced by the mind and are executed. It's where motivation develops. Motivation only leads to action if one believes a possible solution might result. And, that if a solution doesn't come about immediately, the chances of working out eventually will still be increased.

Possibility of It Working Out↑ Motivation↑ Probability of It Working Out↑→It Working Out or Not Working Out→Repeat

The boxing ring of the mind requires a trained, lively,

healthy ego to fight out of it. After all, the reigning champion is the shadow of your mind, which knows everything you've ever thought before. Shadows are amorphous ghosts. An enlivened mind, equipped with a new point of view, is required to defeat the champion. It requires new thoughts that are refined before they can be criticized and possibly beaten down. It requires ideas that are executed before you may change your mind simply because it's a new idea.[25] Get your mind in shape. It won't work with a sluggish mind.

If you're doing drugs, quit them. If you drink, stop drinking. It you smoke, quit smoking. If you're sedentary, get up and start moving. If you're mentally bored, find something new to learn and stimulate yourself with. Try eating healthier. Gauge your health. Feel what it's like to feel good. Sleep as much as you can. Don't feel like a loser if you sleep more than eight hours; the extra throughput you generate after sleeping well more than makes up for the extra hours that you were sleeping. Feel good. Feel healthy. Feel alive. It starts with difficult thinking, and it's worth the effort.

---

25 Of course, there are impulsive ideas that should be reconsidered before they are enacted.

CHAPTER 10: PRIDE, EMBARRASSMENT, SHAME, AND REGRET

Pride, embarrassment, shame, and regret are four intimately related emotions or states of mind, the resolution of which is critically important for one to be at peace with oneself, and enter the transcendental state that is beyond the traditional ego.[26] We have discussed pride before, but someone may feel guilty about feeling proud, because a lot of emphasis is put on people being humble, not showing pride, and not boasting of the things one has done. It's okay to feel pride. In fact, it's essential. Society's taboo against pride and arrogance is partly based on those feelings making others feel bad about themselves.

PRIDE'S BAD RAP

26 This state is not necessary for wellness, but it can be said to be the one step beyond wellness and could be a goal for someone who desires this. Ironically, a total state of nirvana involves no desire whatsoever, even a desire to help others.

Because of pride's bad reputation, we tend to only value or receive it by proxy. We feel the pride from our fathers, mothers, relatives, friends, and so on. Often, the pride of a single person is sought. Typically, for boys, this is the boy's father. A great deal of life energy is spent in the quest of making fathers feel proud. The father typically has very high standards that must be met in order to release his pride to his son. This is usually because the fathers want the sons to be "better than they were." The fathers feel that their accomplishments were not enough, and do not feel prideful themselves. The fathers feel that if they give their sons that extra something that they didn't have, that their sons will "go further than they did" or "be better than they were."

The measuring stick fathers use to decide whether their sons deserve their pride is flawed. They frequently say, "I want him to go further than I did." For sons and fathers who both played baseball, this might entail the father ending his baseball career in high school, and the son going on to play in college. This would be deemed a success. Another measure might be scoring more career points during a high school basketball career. These yardsticks are flawed, because the sons could be doing many other things besides sports. A son could be a better or worse student than the father was, and this extra or lack of studying would certainly impact their success in sports. Would a father be proud of a son who became a high school drop-out, yet managed to play professional ball? Probably.

The father wants to be rewarded vicariously through their son's greater successes, attributable in part to their coaching or helping. The son wants to be rewarded for their hard work and dedication, which is often at a level higher than their father's, by their father's pride. Sometimes this is achieved, and it's a blissful thing. It's a celebratory thing that can be repeated multiple times. Unfortunately, some sons never receive the pride, or even approval, of their fathers. These stubborn fathers may be withholding this approval out of tough love, because they feel that their son doesn't meet their standards, or because they can't feel the emotions to begin with. Ultimately, this leads to a son feeling a lack of love from his father. The son learns that he must earn love, and that love is never given away freely, though nothing could be further from the truth. Every time such a person makes a mistake, he will feel unloved.

My father was always very proud of me. He expressed this profusely, as he did his love for me. Some of these cathartic moments came when he was pretty drunk, but they meant the world to me nonetheless. Part of the reason my dad was like this with me is because he was one of those sons who could never achieve the approval or pride of his own father. He was probably a little too proud of me, and sometimes I felt like I was the Jesus Christ of the universe. The rejections that I faced later in life stung more than they would have if his pride had been more realistic.

I faced a series of rejections during my junior high and high school years in that, no matter what I did, I was cut from both the basketball team and the baseball team. Before this, I played in club teams all year round in baseball, basketball, and soccer. I quit soccer in ninth grade, so that wasn't a problem. I still wanted to play basketball, and especially baseball. From seventh to tenth grade, I was cut from basketball. In ninth and tenth, I was cut from baseball. Before this time, I had the notion in my mind that, if I failed at something, it was simply because I didn't try or do my best. The thought that I might not be good enough, despite doing my best, was chased away very quickly in my mind. I couldn't bear the thought of not being good enough. Each time I was cut, I made up excuses that the coaches were picking favorites or that

I didn't make it because of my reputation in school. This could have been true—I'll never know. Another reason for it was that I didn't emerge from puberty until very late, when I was about sixteen years old. So I was still in a boy's body, competing against peers in more developed bodies. This is actually a very good explanation for why I kept on getting cut, but the fact remains that at the time of the tryouts, despite my best efforts, I wasn't good enough. I remember choking back the tears each time. It now seems like a silly thing to cry about, but my world was crashing at the time.

The only reason I liked baseball so much was because I was a pitcher. There's nothing like being on the mound and pitching well. Pitching not very well is the antithesis of pitching well in every respect, but I don't remember that as much, fortunately. Anyway, in ninth grade I was still pitching for a club team, at fifteen years old. I stood about five foot seven at the time and weighed 120 lbs. I always had a very strong arm, and even at that size, I was throwing fastballs in the low eighties. Baseball fans are obsessed with the speed of fastballs, and so am I, so my biggest regret is not knowing how fast I could've thrown at six foot one, 185 lbs, the size I was in twelfth grade. Would I have thrown in the nineties? I'll never know.

My dad was a baby boomer, and was, like all other baby boomers, riding the wave of a great economy, ample opportunities, and an America that was at its peak in many ways. My dad had many talents, but he only did enough to get by when hard work was required. He was a mediocre student in high school and college, but did manage to secure a college degree. When it came time to utilize his degree and take it to the next level through an internship and enroll in a graduate degree program down south, he declined, because he was too afraid to leave home.

He lived across the street from my grandfather for free in my grandfather's apartment, and remained there until he secured a lucrative union job.

My dad was very dedicated when it came to playing games, sports, and partying, but often shied away from doing real work. My grandfather was a self-made man who came from nothing, the youngest of twelve children whose father died from black lung in the mines when my grandfather was just an infant. His work ethic and desire to improve himself and do things for his family were uncanny. He was married to an equally dedicated, hard-working woman. Together, and individually, they remain the toughest, most durable, and greatest people I have ever known. My dad came from an easier world, so it was impossible for him to have the drive my grandfather did. It was unfair of my grandfather to compare my father to himself, but that was the only yardstick he knew. He was a very hard man in regard to certain matters, and my father's performance and lifestyle were among them.

YOUR STARTING POINT AND YOUR ENDING POINT

Let's consider Figure 10-1 below. The line segment between the dot, birth, and the x, death, represents the progress or path someone made in life. Let's let the length of each segment represent the degree to which the person increased or made his life better. We can easily see that the life on Path B made more progress. What we also know is that Path A and Path B differ in direction. One is pointing up and the other is pointing away to the right at an angle to the other. Path B represents someone born into a privileged life. Their family was upper class. Education was stressed in the early years; they were sent to the best private schools, their parents pulled strings to get them into an Ivy League college, and they eventually become business executive millionaires. The person living life in Path A was born into a poor family. His parents were both alcoholics, and weren't around much. He did not want to have the same lifestyle they did, so he studied hard and became a great student at a terrible public high school. He worked a full time job to pay his way through a community college, and then later went to a university. He was the first college graduate in his family. He became an accountant. Once he started earning a good income, destitute family members started asking him for money. He obliged, and never got paid back. He lived a modest, middle-class lifestyle, and died a happy man.

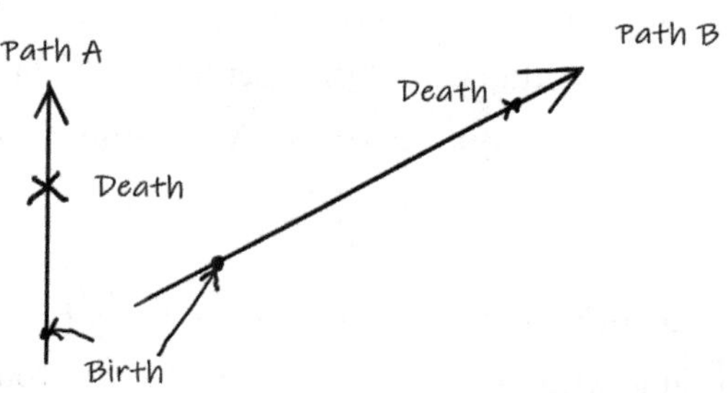

Figure 10-1: Two Life Path Segments

The line segments show that the man who lived Path B went further in life, but the illustration doesn't account for the steepness of the climb. The man who lived through Path A had a steeper climb, and his life was harder. If each path were also measured by elevation gain as well as length, the man on Path A would be judged to have gone further.

What this elaborate example illustrates is that, when seeding our own pride, we can't compare ourselves to others. We do not know the point at which we started relative to others when we are in the middle of our lives comparing them to each other. We may have some idea of where we are at, but we do not know where we will end up. Besides, what measure of comparison, or measures, can really be used to measure the worthiness of a life? Is it your net worth when you die? Ironically, the richest individuals tend to give away their fortunes at the ends of their lives. And the most touching example of a rich man evaluating his life comes from the billionaire Warren Buffet, who said:

> Basically, when you get to my age, you'll really measure your success in life by how many of the people you want to have love you actually do love you.
>
> I know many people who have a lot of money, and they get testimonial dinners and they get hospital wings named after them. But the truth is that nobody in the world loves them.
>
> That's the ultimate test of how you have lived your life. The trouble with love is that you can't buy it. You can buy sex. You can buy testimonial dinners. But the only way to get love is to be lovable. It's very irritating if you have a lot of money. You'd like to think you could write a check: I'll buy a million dollars' worth of love. But it doesn't work that way. The more you give love away, the more you get.

So if the way to get love is to give love, then the most successful lives are the ones who have given the most love away. Remember this the next time you are comparing yourself, your life, to someone else's, or are vying for the pride of someone else so you can love yourself. Give your love away as freely as you wish to receive it. It will come back to you. That person withholding their pride is withholding their love from you because they don't love themselves.

EMBARRASSMENT

The best example of feeling embarrassed is someone walking into the bathroom while you're changing and inadvertently seeing you naked. You yelp, cover up, and feel embarrassed. The person walking in on you feels embarrassed too as they quickly shut the door and retreat. There are societies in Africa and Australia who routinely walk around semi or completely naked and aren't in the least embarrassed. In our society, we are used to being clothed almost all the time. Nakedness is associated with intimacy and extreme privacy. Young children, mostly innocent, parade around naked like Adam and Eve did before they ate the forbidden fruit. At some point, modesty overcomes nakedness. This normally occurs around puberty, when nakedness and private parts become associated with sexual feelings. Sexuality is another thing people in our society tend to be embarrassed about. Americans' sexuality is very repressed. So in this example, embarrassment is literally when someone uncovers or sees a part of you that they weren't meant to see. Figuratively, this is also what embarrassment entails.

PRIDE, EMBARRASSMENT, SHAME, AND REGRET IN SEXUAL ENCOUNTERS

I was at a party by a lake one time when I was a teenager. I was with a pretty girl. Her hand was deformed, probably from a birth defect. It was the size of a toddler's and was not congruent with a normally proportioned hand. I saw her hand but pretended not to notice there was anything unusual. Her hand didn't bother me, nor did I feel like I was engaging in any charity by kissing her. She and I ended up making out, and at one point I touched the hand and felt it touch me. It was different, but I was fine with it. Moments later, another kid pointed at her hand and said, "Dude, what the frick is up with your hand! It's messed up!" The girl shied away in embarrassment. She looked down, dejected and crushed. I should have admonished the boy or something, but I didn't. I didn't say anything. I thought my not saying anything before that was enough, I suppose. Why was the girl not embarrassed to grab me with the hand, but was embarrassed when the boy called it out? Is it because he drew more attention to it? I hope later in life, she became more comfortable with her deformity. I hope that fewer people openly noticed it or rudely pointed it out.

I have a deformity of sorts, but you can't see it. I have a diagnosed major mental illness. It's not the accepted kind: depression or anxiety. It's one of the stigmatized ones, bipolar disorder. Most people think bipolar disorder means you're just moody all the time. That's not the case. The mood changes come in larger cycles, but I will get to that later. Some people know that the more acute version of bipolar disorder can result in hallucinations, delusions, absurd behavior, and forced hospitalizations. This is all true. The people that know this about bipolar look at someone who has been diagnosed with it as "a crazy person" or "someone who's about to go off." Not only that, but also every single negative thing you do is explained away by the illness. "Of course he's mad. He's bipolar." The major mental illnesses—schizophrenia, bipolar disorder, borderline personality disorder, and dissociative identity disorder—are all met with a stigma that equals or exceeds AIDS sufferers in the 1980s. Indeed, people are scared to venture too close to insanity, lest they become infected with it. Therefore I rarely, if ever, tell anyone my diagnosis.[27] The chances that they are knowledgeable about it and accept it are slim. However, I wouldn't feel fully accepted by someone unless they knew of my condition. So while I can hide my deformity, I only rarely feel the sense of acceptance the girl felt when she placed her tiny hand in my giant hand, and I held her hand without hesitation.

How do we arrive at what we consider embarrassing? At some point, an assessment and a choice are made. A choice is made to conceal or ignore what we consider embarrassing about ourselves. Then there are the surprising things we don't know about ourselves, that others point out, that we then feel embarrassed about. Finally, there are the things that other people are embarrassed *for us* about, that we don't even know about. We may be too talkative at parties, and our friend is embarrassed to take us to parties for that reason. She may eventually tell us this, but she may keep it to herself forever. We are oblivious that we are embarrassing at parties.

Embarrassment is a huge part of sexuality in our culture, so I will use yet another example in the setting of passion to illustrate embarrassment. I was preparing to engage in passionate relations with a woman when I was in my late twenties. She was a few years older than me. She was slow to disrobe and was acting rather shy. I asked her, "What is the matter?" She said, "I bet that you are used to looking at the bodies of girls in their early twenties. That's much younger than I am." This was her assumption, because I was a little younger than she was. I assured her that wasn't the case, and that everything would be okay. Her potential embarrassment evaporated away quickly enough to proceed. At some point before this, she had made an assessment that I was

27 Except for everyone reading this book.

used to being with younger women, and that I would unfavorably compare her body to their bodies. She also assumed that, if I did this, I wouldn't take into account that she was older.

There are normally positive feelings associated with having a source of embarrassment revealed and having others accept it. This acceptance is the rain washing some of the dirt off of our faces, because the embarrassment was making us save face. The rain also represents the normal falling of tears, and is the sadness we felt about the embarrassment to begin with, and the future embarrassment that we will continue to face.

Sexual encounters are the ultimate arena for embarrassment. Shame even enters into the equation for these encounters, especially if the sexual encounter was prompted or made possible by intoxicating substances. Shame is when an embarrassing thing, or something that damages our pride or ego, is felt *and* we somehow feel we are responsible for it. Shame differs from guilt in that others are aware of shame but not necessarily guilt. In these sexual encounters, how well you know the person may actually increase or decrease the potential for embarrassment or shame. Unless someone keeps the lights off, you are getting naked in front of each other and engaging each other's intimate areas. Then there's the issue of performance, how good the experience was for each party, and the judgment each party makes of the skills, body, and passions of the other. These judgments may never be stated, but they are there. A first-time sexual encounter is never as good as future encounters could potentially be, when each is more comfortable and more familiar with the other. Then there's how you feel about the encounter afterwards. There could be shame—shame in the thought that you shouldn't have had sex with the person because you didn't know them well enough. There could be shame that you only had sex because you were wasted, or that you just feel dirty in general for doing it. On the other hand, maybe you feel good about your performance or how she finally knows that you have a large member, and you might feel proud. Finally, a friendship might have been ruined because two good friends decided to have sex, and a strong feeling of regret is formed. There you have it: pride, embarrassment, shame, and regret—the subjects of this chapter—all encapsulated by sordid hook-ups.

Shame on me? Shame on You! Shameless

People are embarrassed by different things and to different degrees by those things. Some people aren't really embarrassed by anything. This sounds pretty good, but it can also result in pushing certain people away, losing opportunities, and losing friends. Imagine someone at a formal dinner event using foul language the entire time without a sense of embarrassment. So they keep using the foul language. Potential clients, contacts, and business associates are lost because this person failed to feel embarrassed about something that would embarrass most people. Embarrassment goes hand in hand with certain good manners. If someone tells you that you have bad breath, you should maybe be embarrassed enough that you chew a piece of gum. If someone tells you that there's a piece of asparagus in your teeth, you should be embarrassed enough to remove it.

When there's a disagreement as to what constitutes a shameful act, you may hear someone utter the classic "Shame on you!" When this is said, the recipient rarely feels the shame by virtue of someone else pointing it out. It normally ends up confusing them, and only later, after asking a third party, do they discover what the shame even was. They will then get embarrassed at their ignorance, or they will disagree and shake it off.

When someone feels ashamed of themselves, this feeling immediately leads to regret. Regrets tend to accumulate, like so much baggage. "I regret many things in my life," is a reflective anthem, normally told in a drunken stupor around a fire late at night. People often ask each other what their biggest regret is. This is a great question, because its answer is hard, especially when people say they have many regrets. Have you ever heard someone say, "I regret nothing?" You never hear this, because, in order to erase regrets, a person must forgive themselves for everything. This is very hard to do. Before a person can forgive themselves, they must forgive others. They must forgive others completely. This is also a very hard thing to do, because past transgressions against us hurt.

In the dream heist movie *Inception,* there is a team of dream hustlers that enter people's consciousness via their dreams to steal secrets or plant secret ideas to manipulate those people in real life. So the scenes consist of people asleep in the real world, and the movie shows what's happening in the dream, where the heist is taking place. The people in the dream heist world have to know when they're supposed to wake up, or when they're about to exit the dream. For this a "kick song" is played on headphones on them in the real world. They hear this song in the dream, and know that they're about to wake up. The song that's chosen as the "kick song" is *Non Je ne regrette rien*, by Edith Piaf. The song title means, "No, I regret nothing." This suggests to the viewer that, in order to wake up from a mere dream of life, and to fully live your real life, you have to let go of your regrets. Regrets keep you in the dream of your past. The past is really just a story that we tell ourselves.

In order to let go of your regrets, you have to forgive yourself. In order to forgive yourself, you have to forgive others. In order to forgive others, you have to let go of what they did to you in the past.

People who are shameless are people who have lived in the gutter for so long that they have become desensitized to the immoral, debasing, or underground things that happen in our society. They have resorted to survival mode, or have become drug addicts and the only thing of concern to them any longer is the next fix. Most prostitutes can only endure the shame of their profession because it's a means to obtaining drugs. Strippers justify what they do by the ridiculous amounts of money they make by it, and maybe the real shamed should be the people who waste all of their money just to see women take their clothes off. The embarrassment and shame of nudity is responsible for the entire exotic dancing industry. That is, normally embarrassed and ashamed of their nudity, women would not take their clothes off for sweaty businessmen unless they were paid to do so. I guess this is a good thing.

CHAPTER 11: THAT'S DISGUSTING

Disgust, as we defined in Chapter 2, is an aversion, or a reactive recoil, to a situation, person, smell, sight, sound, taste, or any other thing. The realms of smell, taste, and touch seem to dominate the concept of disgust. There aren't too many disgusting sounds, and something may look ugly, but we rarely say, "That is looking." If someone cannot recoil or get rid of a disgusting stimulus, a feeling of unease, discomfort, or outrage ensues. After these feelings abate, continued exposure to disgust can result in either decreasing or increasing disgust, depending on several variables. Indeed, a tolerance or sensitization always seems to develop from repeated exposure to disgusting things.

A feeling of disgust makes the continuous experience, consciousness of, awareness of, or presence of something increasingly less tolerable. In other words, a disgusting thing makes someone uncomfortable. Disgust is somewhat opposite to comfort, except it's a mere visual, thought, sound, smell, or innuendo that makes someone recoil. Disgust is a reflex, and discomfort is a continuous feeling. It makes someone want to get away from it, not think about it, or get someone to stop presenting it. Why are the same things disgusting to some people but not disgusting to others? Why are these same things not only tolerable to others, but also desirable?

Disgust to some things, like the smell of rotting food or human excrement, is universal. These are hardwired things that prevent us from developing food sickness or other diseases. This is easy to understand. Disgust to things that are culturally driven, age driven, or experience driven are harder to understand. Even though the basics of childbirth are understood by men for years, the actual act and observation of it can cause extreme disgust. Others would label the experience "the miracle of childbirth," "the beauty of childbirth," or simply "part of life." I have been present for three births. At the first one, I was in a sort of terror the entire time, and the delivery was climactic and visceral. At the third birth, I was playing rock and roll music, helping my wife bounce up and down on a birthing ball, and cheering triumphantly during the final pushes, in the same way that I would cheer during a football match. All of the terror was gone, and there was only jubilation...and, still, a little disgust...

We like to think of ourselves as sanitary creatures, free from our biology and basic, animalistic needs. In our cerebral, sanitary world, where many interactions are now remote and digital, merely intellectual and through machines, this is understandable. Even shaking hands with someone who is wearing strong cologne can be disgusting. Shaking the cologne-soaked person's hand, fifty years ago, would probably not be disgusting. It would be more commonplace.

Disgust is strongly related to surprise and novelty. The more used to something a person is, the less likely they are to be disgusted by it. People typically have good manners in public. When treated rudely, we are not used to it, so we recoil in disbelief and disgust. Disgust is a default recoil response to something that is unfamiliar, or that is contrary to prior cultural conditioning. Disgust is like fear, except its goal is to eliminate something that may be offensive or damaging in the long term, as opposed to fear, which acts in response to short-term dangers. We are disgusted by something that smells like poison, and only when we stop to think that it may be poison does fear enter into the equation. Different sexual flavors and acts can elicit disgust in some people and lustfulness in others. Often, the conversion of disgust to other feelings results from repeated exposure to a particular thing, a single exposure to it, or from a detailed mental or physical examination of it. After this, the thing might morph in the mind and be classified as something other than disgusting.

Disgust is always a function of the time it has been familiar to the subject. That is:

Disgust→f(time known)

This function is graphed in Figure 1-3. Note that, in this case, the level of disgust was reduced by time, but a residual level of disgust will always remain. "I originally thought sushi was disgusting. I tried it. It wasn't that good. I ate it again, and learned to like it. I'm still disgusted by the thought of eating raw fish." This figure can also apply to my reaction to witnessing childbirth. I may not ever fully be comfortable with it, but my first word to describe it wouldn't be disgust. It would be described as "intense, overwhelming, and jubilant."

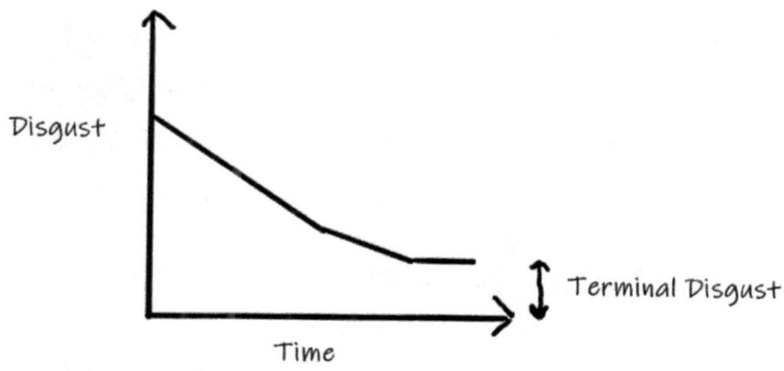

Figure 1-3: Disgust vs Time

As time increases, disgust decreases. The exception to this is if the disgusting thing violates a cultural or sociological norm. In that case, the level of disgust may actually *increase.* This is because the person has more time to continuously compare the disgusting thing to their accepted norms and realize how the disgusting thing conflicts with their beliefs, morals, or religion. The mind contemplates and compares the disgusting stimulus and elevates it to higher offense.

On the other hand, feelings of disgust may decrease with the passage of time. This can be true if a person decides to try something they thought was disgusting but wanted to give a chance anyway, and the experience reinforces what they thought to begin with. For example, oysters are disgusting to many people because they are not accustomed to eating raw seafood. Upon eating it, they may continue to think it's disgusting, or they may decide that they like or love this new foodstuff. How or why that happens is unknown. It's like pondering why some people like some foods versus others.

Disgust then, is a built-in safety measure for protecting against universally disgusting things, such as sewage and decaying animals. It is also there to protect people from unknown things or from things that violate their cultural norms and beliefs. This is an example of the paradigm of primitive man assuming the rustling in the bushes is from a hunting tiger and not merely from the wind although the latter is almost certainly the case.

Disgust = Instinctual aversion to things;

or, Disgust maintains existence while Aversion to New or Culturally Off-Putting Things > Acceptance of New Things or Desire for New Experiences

The desire for novelty, self-improvement, or self-exploration is often the impetus that vanquishes certain feelings of disgust. Also, the prompting of others to explore and share new things also helps confront outstanding feelings of disgust.

There is one aspect of humanity that is universally, at least in our Western culture, initially met with disgust, and is later, at some point accepted as desirable, necessary, or tolerable. This one aspect is introduced at an age where it is not desirable and not pursued, and is then found desirable and pursued at a later point. This is a good thing, because if it wasn't flipped at some point, the human population would decline and eventually our species would become extinct. Of course, I'm referring to sex.

The disgust-to-desirable/tolerable transition regarding sex starts with the first sex ed class or "the birds and the bees" talk from mother and father into late middle age and even into old age. A twenty-year-old would probably never desire the body of a seventy-five-year-old woman, but a seventy-five-year-old man could. There's always something a little dirty, or disgusting, about sex. It's part of what makes it desirable. The contrast between one's sex life and one's regular life is almost unfathomable. Sex is so unlike the rest of our lives and how, with all its barriers, it functions. The ironic thing is that there are sexual advertisements all around us. Why? Because sex sells.

There is nothing stranger than meeting someone, and, hours later, being inside of them or them being inside you. It's certainly disgusting from many standpoints: it's exchanging germs and fluids between two bodies that just encountered each other, it's two people sharing something after only hours of contact that is normally reserved for people with much more mutual familiarity; it's exposure to potential diseases; it's a potential pregnancy that would result in disaster; and it's something that many people will imagine but never do. It's dangerous. The disgust people feel about this situation is the body's recoil response to something that may cause immediate damage. On the other hand, the situation is exciting and desirable. It's meeting someone new. Someone new always appears exciting and beautiful. Earning their trust fast enough that such acts would be permitted and engaged in is a challenge. There are one-night stands that are charming.

To a man, a woman is never again as desirable as when you first see her. In that moment, when you first notice her, your eyes are glued to her and you imagine her being everything she could ever be to you. Because this is a fantasy, she will never quite be what she was to you as when you first saw her. When I was an undergrad, I took an English class where the chairs in the classroom were arranged in a circle. There was a girl who sat directly across from me. She had long brown hair, a beautiful face, and was very tall. She was slender but appeared athletic. In that moment when I first noticed her, it was perfection. I imagined her and I being in some impossible romance and her bringing out the best in me, latent things that I never knew existed but blossomed like seasonal flowers. I ended up becoming her friend. No romance ever developed, but I had a secret crush on her and always thought she was beautiful. I spent a lot of time right next to her. Fortunately, her beauty and my attraction kept on fading the more I got to know her. The more I realized she was just a human like I was. I talked to her as much as I could, to stop liking her. I even started arguing with her to see her mean side. It worked, a little. I was relieved when we went our separate ways. She actually reentered my life a few years later when I was in a rough spot, and ended up being a good friend—a great friend actually. However, I couldn't get over my romantic feelings that were still there for her. I tried kissing her and was rejected. It was one of the only times I ever tried to kiss someone and they turned away from me. She was, perhaps, disgusted in some way by me.

Sex at a young age is dangerous, undesirable, and would have no biological purpose. Perhaps that's why children are universally disgusted by the thought of it. That's a good thing. Imagining having sex with someone you don't know or barely know is also disgusting, mostly. That's also a good thing, because it protects us. Sleeping with someone who is promiscuous is disgusting. That protects you from a potential STI.

After finding safe sexual partners and becoming more experienced sexually, people tend to become fully comfortable with their own anatomy, and with their partner's anatomy. At this point in life they are more likely to turn to sex acts or practices that they used to find disgusting. They will do this to replicate the thrill they originally felt from normal—now boring sex. These are the long term couples that visit the sex shop, try new positions, play sex games, experiment with different types of sex, and even engage in more scandalous behavior like "swinging," visiting strip clubs together, or inviting others into their bedrooms.

A man may witness childbirth and feel weird about penetrating her vagina after she recovers. "A baby came out of there. Now,

I'm supposed to put my penis back in there?" All fathers know the feeling. Eventually, you learn it's all part of life. The fact that so many aspects of our sexuality are taboo, are behind closed doors most of the time, and infringe on various religions make it difficult to accept. There is the realization that humans are part animal, and are driven by reproductive urges. Fortunately, for us, sex is linked to love, pleasure, and disgust. There are a host of hormones in our body that control how disgusted or attracted we are to certain people or sexual situations, and when we are disgusted and when we are attracted. The endocrine system is a complex system, and how it regulates sex and desire is extremely complex. A good portion of your sex drive is controlled by this system. However, another portion is driven by your mind. The mind is the ultimate aphrodisiac and the thing that turns disgust into lust.

Now, there are certain sexual things that start out as desirable and decline to disgusting. Let's take kissing, for example. The following is actually proven by surveys and things like that. In the beginning of a relationship, a good amount of time is spent kissing. A good amount of time is spent tasting each other. There are many hidden things going on here that are mostly driven by biology that we still don't fully understand. The taste of someone and how that ignites you to further kiss them and do other things is related to how biochemically compatible you are with each other. Similarly, the way you smell to each other, even if you aren't consciously aware of each other's natural scent, strongly determines how attracted you are to someone. This could be what's meant by "having chemistry." Indeed, there is a lot of hidden chemistry going on: pheromones, scents, body language, and other animalistic things. After you have been together a while, your relative tastes, in literal and hidden ways, have become known, both consciously and unconsciously. Couples who have been together longer do not kiss nearly as much as new ones, and may even be disgusted by deep tongue kissing. Once in a while, during sex, or at other passionate moments, a tongue kiss may be delivered, but it's short lived and timed appropriately. Oral sex also tends to have this trend. Again, it's a matter of someone getting their taste of someone, and then refraining after that taste has been acquired.

What's the opposite of disgust? Is it like? No, that doesn't quite fit. The opposite would be a feeling of wanting something without quite knowing why, wanting to do acts that the rational mind might consider disgusting, and the pursuit of doing these things. One opposite of disgust is lust. Lust makes you do things that might damage you in the short term. Lust makes you expose yourself and make yourself vulnerable. Lust can become disgust, just like disgust can become lust. If you encounter someone you think is undesirable, you may say that "they're disgusting." If you lust after someone, you make the language pretty and say "she's hot" or "he's a handsome man." Lustful feelings are euphemized. You would never say, "I want to shove my tongue into his mouth and move it around." That sounds disgusting. You'd say, "I want to passionately kiss him." There's a love factor, even in lust. Things are prettied up. There are courtesies you take when you are merely "having sex" with someone. We dress up lust. We bust on the things we disgust.

It may be disgusting, but the opposite of disgust is lust.

CHAPTER 12: ADDICTION ATTRITION

In Alcoholics Anonymous, Al-anon, Narcotics Anonymous, gambling support groups, sex addiction therapy, and while attending other programs that are attempting to treat addiction, we hear a familiar phrase: "addiction is a disease." For some reason, labeling alcoholism as a disease makes people feel better while they are watching Lenny piss his paycheck away every week at the bar and rendering himself too broke to support his family. It makes people feel better watching Melissa being addicted to meth for so long that her teeth fall out, her once-beautiful appearance withers, and she eventually dies while squatting in an abandoned warehouse. We can't possibly fathom why someone would continuously destroy their life with something so obviously detrimental. So we put a label on it. We call it a disease. A disease is something you randomly acquire, or get infected by through another person passively. A disease is something you're born with. You never choose a disease. In every form of addiction, a conscious choice is made. Therefore, addiction cannot be a disease. If you accept it as an incurable disease, you will never believe that you can overcome it. If you accept addiction as a disease, you will accept that you have the disease and won't do anything to quit the real source of the addictive behavior—as we shall see.

I used to drink to the extent that, by some modern definitions, I would be considered at least a problem drinker. It was mostly weekend binge drinking, and then in my later drinking career there was some weekday drinking. It never impacted my ability to go to school or to work. It did negatively affect my life, and I can only see that now because I quit drinking many years ago.

Let's forget that for now though. Let's go back in time to when I first starting drinking. I got a hold of booze, one way or another, and, when I was drunk, *I liked the way I felt.* That's it. That's why I liked to drink. As I continued to drink, the buzzes began to fade and didn't feel nearly as good as they first had. This is a traditional pattern of drinking or drug use. The high wearing off over time. It applies to drinking as it does to drugs. The first years of drinking often resulted in euphoria. As time progressed, there was less euphoria, and more of a calming effect, an anxiolytic effect. Drinking some beers after working hard all day took the edge off. As I got a little older, my personality became a little more anxious. I wasn't sheltered by high school or college. I was out in the real world. I was worried a lot. In my head, I said *I drink because I like to get fucked up.* However, the reality was that I couldn't tolerate how I felt when I was sober, and the booze was like medication for those anxious feelings. Again, another common pattern: self-medicating. That said, there are two reasons—and the only two reasons—that addiction ever exists and propagates unmitigated. Addiction is never impossible to stop. Here are the two reasons why someone is addicted to anything:

1. The behavior or use is undertaken to feel positive feelings one believes one cannot feel without the behavior or use.
2. The behavior or use is undertaken to remove negative feelings one believes one cannot remove without the behavior or use.

In other words, people do drugs to get high, which feels good, because they can't feel that high without the drugs. A bored housewife may find that shopping gives her a "high," and soon finds herself pulling out her credit card more and more often for a renewed boost. A man with social anxiety may drink to remove his anxiety so he can talk to people at a party; this is a problem if drinking is the only way he feels comfortable socially. Someone snorts cocaine to feel like they can do anything in the world, and they ramble on about plans that only result in a few scribbled lines. College students can't study, focus, and get good grades, so they take Adderall to focus. Problematic gamblers may gamble to feel alive; the possibly of losing thrills them so much so that, even when they lose, they feel just as alive as they do when they win. It's a literal lose-win that's a win-win.

Therefore, the solution to addiction is super simple: learn to feel what the addiction makes you feel without the substance or behavior and learn to naturally eliminate the unwanted feelings that the addiction drowns, vaporizes, smokes, gambles, or copulates away.

When you hear someone say, "I'm on a natural high," you're likely to roll your eyes. Even though I know it's true, I think it sounds dumb, and as if the person is bragging. You may not believe me, but it's possible to enter transcendental states, altered states of consciousness, psychedelic states, and enduring feelings of blissfulness that put the best drugs to shame. There was a famous experiment where a group of monks tried LSD. When asked how it was they said, "It was nice, but it was nothing compared to meditation." If the monks were less polite, they would be scoffing at a drug that many consider "hardcore" and would gloat that they could exceed that state just by closing their eyes. I'm not a meditation expert, but I have experienced the psychedelic and blissful states of meditation. I have felt my chakra system light up like a Christmas tree. I have felt my life force transfer into and out of another. I have had rapturous feelings sitting there doing nothing but contemplating and reflecting on the nature of God and life. I feel bad for people who don't have bipolar disorder and who have never experienced mania. They have never experienced their entire body orgasming simultaneously in concert while feeling like their head was on fire and it was about to explode. I have to take drugs so I don't trip; normal people take drugs to trip. How's that for irony?

It's funny how many addictions there are that are not referred to as diseases. They are considered bad habits, unwanted behavior, things to avoid, and so on. On the other hand, some addictions are actually encouraged even when they are damaging for the person engaging in the behavior. Addiction to spending and consumerism is encouraged by our materialistic society that now permits shopping at any time via the internet. Workaholism is considered a positive behavior because it can increase personal income (to buy more things) and to increase corporate profits. Addiction to prescribed painkillers is beneficial to those that sell such drugs.

Addictions classified as diseases normally have to have the power to completely ruin your life or the lives of your family and loved ones. With these addictions, the person with the "disease" confesses that they have no **ability to even address** the addiction, or the person with the disease confesses that they have no

desire to quit the addiction. I am going to make a new classification for addictions: Addiction is a disease insofar as a person is *lovesick because of it.* Addiction is a lovesickness. Addiction is only conquered if the love for it is permanently destroyed. It's a bad breakup that takes a long time.

I spoke to some people who used to smoke crack. They explained to me how getting high on crack felt, and how much they *loved it.* They said that even though they didn't smoke it anymore, that they would *love* to, if they could only get the chance, and that their love for it will never waver, as long as they're alive, even though they might never get to smoke it again. While telling me this, these people had the look of love and tender affection in their eyes. Their voices inflected and croaked with love and longing. It was as if they were describing a long past love that they lost. This is exactly what they were describing. Even if you quit an addiction for the rest of your life, if you still love it, and yearn to do it, then you are not over the addiction. It still has power over your emotions, and it still has power over you because thinking about it can change the way you feel.

I spoke to a lot of alcoholics. Some of them quit drinking through the cultish Alcoholics Anonymous. Alcoholics Anonymous forces you to admit that you'll always be an alcoholic, that you're powerless against your disease, and that you need to participate in AA to keep on not drinking. Basically, AA gets you addicted to AA in place of alcohol. So, I guess these people should be considered "recovering alcoholics," as the system proclaims that they will always be alcoholics, as a person with cancer is never cured, but in remission if they don't have the cancer anymore. Here are the first two steps of AA:

1. We admitted we were powerless over alcohol—that our lives had become unmanageable.

2. Came to believe that a Power greater than ourselves could restore us to sanity.

The twelve steps of AA have six direct or indirect references to God. I guess that means "good luck" to anyone who is an alcoholic but does not believe in God. The Steps also require you to confess your sins, write out everyone you ever wronged, and try to right all of the wrongs you did to people. If you drank for eighteen years, drunkenly beat your wife every night, spent all your money on booze so your family lived in squalor, how could you make that up to them? Remember, the classic booze infatuation begins with *I like getting fucked up.*

Almost all of the recovering alcoholics I talked to still loved booze. All they did in their mind was make a simple substitution, a trick almost, that the benefits of not boozing outweighed the benefits of boozing. This was an equation:

Stop Drinking = Benefits of quitting booze > benefits of boozing

This occurs when a person realizes they are heading for a premature death due to the ill health effects of alcohol, that they are losing touch with family, or that they can't afford to booze anymore. For example, they may be developing cirrhosis of the liver or have found out that they have Hepatitis C. In this case, the medical disease stopped the addiction—it didn't create it. This is true for many addictions. A meth addict will start to develop serious health ailments, diseases, in response to the meth. The meth addict may become scared sober by the fact that meth will kill them if they keep on using it. This is also an equation:

Stop smoking crystal meth = Fear of Death > Fondness of Getting High

Turning the philosophy of addiction on its head, it's clear that medical diseases stop or even prevent addiction-classified as diseases rather than addiction being an isolated disease. The child of an alcoholic who died of cirrhosis of the liver refuses to ever take a drink, lest she "turn out like my mom did." This is disease preventing addiction from ever starting. When I quit drinking, the biggest reason was because I had developed bipolar disorder, and it was then necessary to quit drinking to sustain wellness. There are numerous accounts of people quitting drugs, booze, or other things because they developed a disease.

Let's return to the recovering alcoholic. As you get him to speak about boozing, a far off glint appears in his eyes, and you can tell he's either imagining himself boozing or remembering himself boozing. He starts recollecting booze stories, or even directly says "...wish I was still boozing." Recovering alcoholics should be called lovesick alcoholics. They're still in love with booze. These alcoholics are always prone to going back to the booze, because they still love it. This is like trying to get over an ex when you're still lovesick over them. You have to fall out of love with an addiction to cure it. This is extremely hard, because, like a bad boyfriend, the addiction has given you a lot of love, mixed in with a lot of bad. It's a perfectly mixed drink.

A vision for the future that is comprised of equating pleasure multiplied by duration for both sobriety and continued drug use is sufficient to start quitting an addiction. For example, one may imagine oneself feeling healthy and happy, without drugs, in the future, for an indefinite period of time after quitting. The drug user has already become attached to high levels of pleasure for relatively short durations. Conversely, equating enduring a bad feeling for a spell to the release of it after a period of time can also effect an attempt to quit an addiction. In other words, an addict will benefit from the fading of withdrawal symptoms before they experience the natural, positive pleasures that are available to a nonuser. The mindset of someone eliminating an addiction for the pleasure it gives goes like this:

Natural Pleasure x Time > Addiction Pleasure x Time ; Only When Time > critical time

These inequalities are saying that eventually the overall natural pleasure without the addiction will exceed the shorter, but more intense, pleasure given by the addiction. However, the inequality recognizes that it will take a critical time before this is the case. That critical time is the time between when one makes the conscious decision to end the addiction until the time that they are likely to have permanently quit the addiction. The vision of a better future, of how it will be after the critical time is reached, is paramount for quitting. The vision of the future should be positive, and a firm realization that you're better off without the addiction. The vision of the future shouldn't be that the positive effects of quitting outweigh the positive effects of not quitting. It should be that your natural being, your ability to feel positive feelings, your ability to feel pleasure, and become a better, healthier person is enhanced permanently by quitting the addiction. You fall in love with this better self, and dump your old, addicted self. The lovesickness disappears. This is the way to permanently eliminate addiction, rather than merely suppress it.

I have quit smoking several times before. It took me three tries to accomplish it. Typically, the hardest day of quitting cold turkey is on Day 3, because that's the day nicotine is completely out of your body. I remember my Day 3s distinctly. On this day, my entire body erupted with desire for cigarettes and smoking. I knew what a real craving was like, and I finally understood why it was so hard to quit smoking. To reinforce my desire to quit and get over this hump, I thought of how I would be after I completely quit smoking. I had read the benefits of quitting smoking and some of the "side effects" of quitting smoking. The "side effects" were really just your body returning to its natural, healthier state. I remember my mouth having so much saliva that I frequently had to spit. Increased salivary production is a benefit of quitting smoking, and it's one of the things that makes nonsmokers' teeth healthier. I smelled my fingers and clothes, and relished that they didn't smell like cigarettes. As the days went by, I kept on noticing more things. The sensation in my fingers became stronger as my circulation improved. After two weeks of not sleeping from the nicotine withdrawal, I started sleeping like a baby, and I dreamt more. I had more energy. Food regained some flavor. My sense of smell increased, and so on. It was easy to see that my natural experience of life all the time, with these regained functions, was better than my state with cigarettes and the temporary release I got from them. I loved how I felt. I fell in love with my new self. This happened every time I quit an addiction, and every time I chose to engage in a new, healthy habit.

Quitting other addictions, such as hard drugs, sex addiction, gambling, and shopping, is more complicated because there are personality, mood, and family histories that enter into the equation of why people with these addictions feel they need the drugs or behavior to take away the hurt or to feel happy. While these addictions may be more complicated, trying to treat the addictions directly is like cutting weeds. The addictions will grow back, because the roots are still there. I don't have personal direct experience with drug addiction, gambling, or shopping addiction. However, I have probably engaged in behavior that some would consider sex addiction, and I could be described as a workaholic. Being a workaholic is accepted, and even sometimes encouraged, by society. Workaholism produces a greater amount of what our capitalistic society is based on, so it's not looked upon as an addiction or even as a bad habit. Nevertheless, workaholism is detrimental to one's health, self-esteem, family, and overall well-being.

As I said, I might have been diagnosed as a sex addict in the earlier years of my life. Coincidentally, my father could have been diagnosed this way too. The sins of the father are the sins of the son. I have a potential excuse for this behavior, but I won't take it.[28] As a young kid, I was good at a lot of things, including sports, academics, and even at making friends. Adults loved me, and I even ended up going on vacations with other relatives and families. There is a hidden knife to being good at things. When you fail at the things you are good at, it is catastrophic. This is how I felt when I was cut from the teams I described in Chapter 10.

Even as a young boy, girls always liked me. I remember girls coming up to me with letters stating how their friend liked me, and other puppy-love things. This evolved with age and hormones. I was never at a loss for a girlfriend or a romantic figure in my life. To a young man, and even to men in general, the pursuit of women, the courtship of women, the possibility of women, sex stories, sexual prowess, and beautiful women are all integral to a man's sense of his own manliness and self-worth. How women were attracted to me and how I interacted with them caused an ego supernova, combined with all the emotions that romantic passions naturally bring. I was addicted to it. But I was in love with *myself* when I was doing all of these things. I wasn't in love with the addiction. This description of "being in love with myself when I was dating someone" is a description of lustful, transient love. I was basically extending this normally

---

28 Bipolar mania results in hypersexuality.

transient feeling. I wasn't consciously doing it. I was just taking the opportunities that were bestowed upon me. The girls sometimes got their feelings hurt, but these same girls, now women, would probably laugh now, reflecting upon such feelings. I also sometimes got my feelings hurt, which seemed critical at the time but now, in my adult mind, these feelings were merely juvenile. As I got older, I eventually settled down with one person, and this behavior ceased.

However, I'm not sure how I'd act if young, beautiful women began throwing themselves at me again, for whatever reason. This is the situation faced by powerful politicians, athletes, and celebrities. They tend to take the opportunities that are bestowed upon them. When they get caught, a big fuss is made out of the behavior. Some say that they are sex addicts. They enroll in therapy for this to save face. To be honest with you, I think they're just taking advantage of being able to extend the thrill that I had experienced in my young adult life in their older adult lives. If you've ever watched the show *Temptation Island*, you know that how faithful someone is depends just as much on how severely they are tempted than on how faithful they actually are. That said, sex addiction doesn't exist. It's just someone exploiting a, quite literally, desirable situation.

Okay, so let me get even bolder. Let's talk about gambling. Gambling exploits a mental conditioning in people whereby a reward is presented at random intervals where intervals can be controlled by the frequency by which a person attempts to obtain a reward. To imagine this, picture someone at the slot machine pulling the lever mechanically until they hit a mini-jackpot. This type of reward structure creates the highest intensity to seek a reward. A gambler may be someone who is averse to hard work, is impatient, is impulsive, and is a natural thrill seeker. Finally, a gambling addict is typically bad at statistics and has little to no knowledge of the probabilities of gambling. A gambler is an addict manufactured by a personality that is surrounded by things that exploit his personality's weaknesses. Gambling is also society's fault. Any form of gambling, where the house has more favorable long terms odds, should be illegal, because, across the board, it's taking everyone's money by duping them into thinking they can get rich quick.

A shopping addict is actually shopping for some real feelings that she is missing in her life. She may be missing attention, love, recognition, and self-respect. The thrill of buying the material things temporarily fills this void. Also, our society promotes shopping, materialism, and always buying the next new thing.

Drug addicts are continuously shortcutting to obtain good feelings and to shed bad ones. Their inability to feel good things normally goes very deep, and their career as a drug addict often reinforces this. They often have some bad event, or events, like people dying in their life, and they are taking drugs to numb the pain.

Despite my words in this chapter, I feel compassion and sympathy for all addicts and all programs that attempt to help such people. I have lost friends and loved ones to addiction. Most people I know have a crutch or two, even if it's as innocuous as junk food. These crutches won't be eliminated by replacing them with new ones, or by other hands holding you up. The crutches will be eliminated by throwing the crutches away and standing on your own two feet. You can seek help in doing this, but in the end, it's your choice, and your choice alone. You need to fall out of love with the addiction and love a potentially better self.

CHAPTER 13: TO ERR IS HUMAN

The title of this chapter is from the famous quote by Alexander Pope:

To err is human; to forgive, divine.

On one hand, divinity involves direct forgiveness. In this case, the one granting forgiveness is God or Jesus, or some other religious figure. In an intercession, a third party prays for someone to God. In the intercession of the saints, for example, one prays to a saint, who is thought to send these prayers directly to God. Some doctrines also believe that it is possible to pray through people who are dead, but who have been "saved in Christ." In any event, forgiveness may be sought through these third parties, along with God or Jesus.

The other hand of forgiveness is people acting divinely through forgiveness. That is, people forgiving the sins of others. This doctrine is so important, that it's included in the Lord's Prayer:

"This, then, is how you should pray:

"'Our Father in heaven,

hallowed be your name,

your kingdom come,

your will be done,

on earth as it is in heaven.

Give us today our daily bread.

And forgive us our debts,

as we also have forgiven our debtors.

And lead us not into temptation,

but deliver us from the evil one.'

—Matthew 6:9-13, NIV

THE PRICE OF GOD'S FORGIVENESS

In the statement "And forgive us our debts, as we also have forgiven our debtors," debts and debtors are essentially sins and sinners. This statement carries the weight of the golden rule behind it. The golden rule would have one forgiving others because one would want to be forgiven by others. Instead, the Lord's Prayer invites God the Father to forgive sins if one has forgiven others. Indeed, this invitation is like a bonus to following the golden rule, especially since God's forgiveness is certainly worth more than a person's forgiveness, right?

Not exactly. In Christianity, it is stated in various passages that God's penchant for forgiveness is infinite. There is no sin that is unforgiveable. To obtain forgiveness, all one has to do is admit that one has sinned, and then ask for forgiveness. This admission should be followed with remorse and perhaps a commitment (probably to be broken again) to not doing it again. Admitting to sin is very difficult sometimes. "I didn't do anything wrong" is the common mantra. So God's formula for forgiveness is simple:

God's Forgiveness = Admission of Sin + Remorse for Sin + Promise to try to not do it again + Asking for Forgiveness

Remorse for Sin + Promise to try to not do it again is another way of saying *repenting from one's sins.* It was just broken up into two parts for clarity.

THE PRICE OF HUMAN FORGIVENESS

This formula is not followed by individuals. Many people hold grudges, and many people love to hold grudges. They hold grudges above someone's head for an indefinite period of time, and these grudges dictate how this someone will be thought of or treated for a long time to come, perhaps for a lifetime. As one becomes older, one's heart tends to harden. This is from the accumulation of grudges, guarding one's heart from future harm in response to past harms, and a justified belief that people won't change the way they are. The hardened people are dealing with hardened people. As such, the propensity for either one of them changing is lower than if they were younger. It's not impossible for older people to change, it's just harder; they have more momentum. An object in motion tends to stay in motion. As someone takes a certain life direction, they tend to continue to move in that direction. Figure 13-1 illustrates this concept.

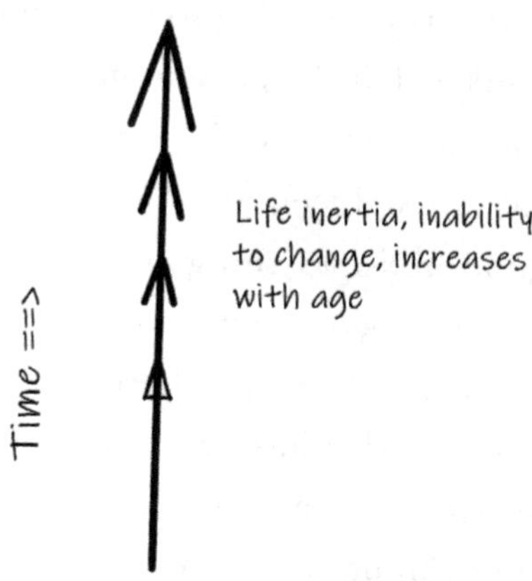

Figure 13-1: Life Inertia with Time

I know too many family members, some in my own family, who have written each other off for good because of one trespass, or a series of trespasses. Some of these write-offs are from an inability to forgive. Others are because they don't want their lives damaged anymore by these people. Finally, there are some that are a combination of these. The inability to forgive also stems from one thinking that forgiveness needs to lead to the other person changing their behavior, or changing who they are. Of course, this trespasser may promise to change and may fail to do so. Or, they will be more realistic, and will flat out refuse to change. The person can still forgive the other person and accept that they will keep on engaging in hurtful behavior. So, there's the other option: completely forgiving the person, becoming at peace with them, but deciding to keep them at a distance or outside of their lives.

The most tragic of these forgiveness scenarios is when one of these people dies before either of them can forgive each other. This leads to regrets such as, "If only he were still around, I'd tell him I was sorry for being so hard on him." The underscore of these thoughts is that the person only developed the ability to ask for forgiveness in the time since death. Unlike when a dog dies, there's always mixed feelings when a person dies. You remember both the good and bad things the person has done to you and others. Out loud, people tend to only speak of the good things, but inside their heads it's a different story. When a dog dies, it's a complete loss. A dog has never wronged anyone. I've felt guilty about being sadder when dogs have died than when people have died. I'm sure I'm not the only one who has felt this way.

AFFORDING HUMAN FORGIVENESS

Whenever someone hurts someone, the other person says something like, "They should have known better!" This saying is such a cliché that when someone is accused of it, they reflexively say, "You're right, I should have known better." Why should they have known better? They should have known better because someone is looking at their behavior and thinking, "If he hadn't screwed me over, I wouldn't be hurting right now. Therefore, he shouldn't have screwed me over." There's a critical assumption in this statement. They are assuming the purpose of the person's action was merely to screw them over. In some cases, this is true, but normally the person got screwed over by the infinite world of unintended consequences. So the offending person says, "I didn't mean to screw you over, I was just trying to save some money." The other person is now in a position to either accept that statement or go back to their first one. If they accept the statement, they may be on the path to forgive the person.

Let's examine a situation where someone decides to deliberately screw somebody over. I'm sure they had perfectly good reasons for wanting to screw the other person over. Maybe in their opinion, the other person deserved it. Maybe they didn't, and this person just wanted to feel the satisfaction of preserving their ego. In any case, they had reasons for doing it; otherwise, they wouldn't have done it, right? Should they have known better? Better is relative; the alternative of not having done it is better to the person who got screwed over. After all, they are the ones that got screwed over. They experienced nothing positive out of it. But, it was better to the person who did it. Maybe the victim, saying, "He should have known better," should know better than to say that, because they should know that it was better for him to screw them over.

Here's the more poignant question: "Could he have known better?" Was the possibility and capability in him and in his heart to not have screwed them over? This is actually asking, "Did he have a choice?" If somebody punches you in the face, you might reflexively punch them back. There's an element of choice in it; perhaps you could have stopped yourself from hitting back. Maybe not, though. Some behaviors are so ingrained that responses become reflexive. If you cut someone off on the freeway, they, without thinking, may cut you off in revenge.

Picture a child looking at a stove burner heating up. The burner changes to red as it heats up, as we all know. The child is curious regarding the color change, so he reaches up and gets burned by the burner. He cries in agony. Do we chastise the child for hurting himself? Of course not. *He couldn't have known any better. He was curious, as any child would be.* In life, we are not much different than children. We are constantly encountering new situations, new people, and new dilemmas. If we act in one way, and it ends up that someone doesn't like it, how is it possible that we could have known better? This goes back to truth and weighing choices. The outcome of every single choice would have to be known and the infinite consequences of each known and correctly evaluated. There's no way that anyone could know better. This is why God possesses infinite forgiveness. There is no right choice or wrong choice. There is simply the best choice that you know at the time. My grandfather used to always say:

I try to be the best man that I know how to be.

This is a noble statement, but within it, there are severe limitations. It says "...that I know how to be." This knowledge is based on a finite life, and a finite amount of resources. The resources are things like time, energy, effort, money, patience, other people, and chance, which is the unknown. Also, in saying "I try..." this is admitting that there are times when he could have, but did not, put the maximum amount of effort toward being the best man that he knew how to be. Yoda said, "No! Try not! Do, or do not. There is no try." This statement connotes two things. First, that when you set out to do something, you are saying what you are doing and are not immediately considering the possibility that you could not do it. It's also stating that, after you do something, you recognize exactly what you did. Instead of saying, "I tried to lift the ship out of the swamp, but I didn't lift the ship out of the swamp because the ship was too big," you would say, "I didn't lift the ship out of the swamp because I didn't believe that I could do it." So, a more virtuous version of my grandfather's mission would be:

I be the best man that I know how to be.

This is the same statement, with the limitations of "...That I know how..." except that it implies the maximum effort will be expended in being the "...best man..." In considering himself in a single moment, he could have said:

I am the best man that I knew how to be.

And, on his deathbed, possibly the least regretful bedside life confession ever:

I had been the best man that I knew how to be.

But, in that confession, the entire statement hinges on "that I knew." I think we all think we are trying to be the best people we *can be*, but we all end up trying to be the best people we *know how to be.* The best of us be the best people we know how to be. We shouldn't have known better because we couldn't have known better. We're eighty years swimming in thirty billion years, assuming that the ultimate age of the universe will be twice what it is now. The duration of this swim is like an eighty-year-old holding his breath underwater for seven seconds.

COULDN'T HAVE KNOWN BETTER

Once you realize that people couldn't have known any better, then it is easy to forgive them. You're forgiving the child who burned his hand on the stove. You're forgiving someone who didn't do anything wrong to begin with. You're alleviating their guilt at no expense to you. It's hard to accept that people don't know any better, but recall all the times you made a choice where you were doing your best, not trying to harm anyone, and you ended up having to beg for someone's forgiveness. Forgiveness from God wasn't enough, forgiveness from the other person was necessary. Despite God being a Supreme Being, forgiveness from others is more important.

IT IS FORGIVE AND FORGET

True forgiveness isn't accepting an apology and keeping the trespass in your mind constantly. Having it torment you after saying you forgive is no different than not forgiving at all. To benefit from the wash of forgiveness, you must also forget the transgression. It's impossible for it to completely fade from memory, but it will be water under the bridge if you let it go and stop thinking about it. You have to forget in order to forgive, and you must forgive in order to forget.

THE REAL REASON FORGIVENESS IS SO IMPORTANT

So it's evident that divine forgiveness makes us feel better about ourselves and enables us to live our lives without as much guilt. It's clear now that the forgiveness of others is harder to obtain, and this forgiveness allows others to move forward in their lives, and even be together with family and friends again.

There's still a question though—why is there so much focus on forgiveness in the Bible and in other places? The answer is clear. People hold many regrets, self-hatred, and other negative thoughts about themselves for the sins they committed against themselves. These are the times they didn't perform as they wanted to, let the love of their life pass by, they missed out on that perfect job, or chose not to move to California. These regrets and self-inflicted sin destroy a person from the inside out. How can you forgive yourself? Do you have to forgive yourself? Well, if there are things you did or didn't do in the past that are causing you misery, and you have regrets, that's the very definition of sin. The hardest person to receive forgiveness from is yourself.

Once you obtain forgiveness from God, you get and give forgiveness from others, and then, finally, you learn how to forgive yourself. You realize that you didn't know any better. You realize that you couldn't have known any better. You burned yourself on the stove, but you learned not to touch it afterwards. Your only sin was not knowing better, and there's no way that you could have known better. Therefore, you committed no sin. Forgive yourself, unload your burden of the past, and be quick to forgive others.

CHAPTER 14: RELAX

The pursuit of relaxation is the avenue that leads to many addictions. Indeed, relaxation for some people, or the absence of stress, can only be felt by the introduction of a cigarette, a joint, a beer, or a glass of wine. The habitual use of these substances can lead to addiction. Smoking cigarettes or marijuana is not really considered serious addiction. Drinking can certainly be, but only if it exceeds a certain amount.[29] Why is this? Because relaxing without something like alcohol is extremely difficult. A text I read on acupuncture said that total relaxation in today's society might be impossible.

In Chapter 2, we discussed nervousness. Relaxation is essentially the absence of nervousness, perhaps mixed in with some comfort. This is why a popular liquor is called Southern Comfort.

Relaxation = *Comfort/Nervousness; Comfort>0*

---

29 And the alcohol Gods have determined that this is such a small amount that many casual drinkers are actually problem drinkers or alcoholics. Regardless, many of them are drinking just to relax.

This simple equation shows that as nervousness increases, relaxation decreases; they are said to be "inversely proportional." If nervousness becomes very small, relaxation can grow very large. Indeed, the equation suggests that if nervousness reaches zero, then relaxation can approach infinity. This is because any number divided by zero can be said to be equal to infinity. However, one must be reasonably comfortable in order to relax. That said, if comfort is equal to zero, which just means the person is uncomfortable (a very common occurrence), then relaxation is equal to 0/0, which can be said to be equal to 1. If a person is uncomfortable, but not very nervous, then their relaxation is at 0, because comfort = 0, and 0 divided by any number is zero.

Obviously, in order to be relaxed, one must both be comfortable and not nervous. Not nervous is a poor description to describe the absence of nervousness, so let's introduce some terms, in decreasing order of nervousness, to describe diminishing phases of nervousness.

Nervousness in Decreasing Order = Calm > Placid > Peaceful > Tranquil > Serene

These all words mean basically the same thing, and their ranking were derived from my subjective evaluation of their uses in context. There is a particular mantra in a meditation video I have listened to that goes like this:

Love manifests beauty

Contentment expresses tenderness

Tenderness begets humility

Humility creates compassion

And compassion creates tranquility

Love, Love manifests beauty

If you have a feeling of love in your heart, the world around you appears beautiful. Beauty puts people at ease, and makes them feel comfortable, or content. Someone who is content is open to subtle feelings, and can feel the feelings of others. Sympathetic feelings tend to diminish one's preoccupation with oneself, resulting in humility. Humility, a low focus on oneself, permits compassionate feelings for others to develop. Compassion can be a general feeling directed to the universe in general and doesn't have to be expressed just person to person. Compassion is feelings that are not concerned with you, and when you're not focused on yourself, a state of tranquility develops. Going through this process many manifest in more love, which will manifest more beauty. And this cycle can continue. This mantra illustrates a path towards tranquility combined with becoming internally comfortable with yourself and simultaneously compatible with the universe. Feeling comfortable within and without may be the ultimate comfort—serenity in my list above. Speaking of serenity, let's examine the classic serenity prayer:

God, grant me the serenity to accept the things I cannot change,
Courage to change the things I can,
And wisdom to know the difference.

This prayer is used extensively in Alcoholics Anonymous, which I discussed in Chapter 12. Accepting the things you cannot change is akin to developing feelings of compassion and humility. Changing the things you can results in satisfaction, which results in contentment (at least for a while). The wisdom to know the difference makes one comfortable, as in being comfortable knowing when to act and when to not act. A wise man is comfortable in that he tends to know what to do, when to do it, and when to not do anything. When someone starts a new job, they are very uncomfortable and nervous, because they do not know what to do. When people always know what to do, they tend to stay in their comfort zones.

Worrying is thinking about something important with an uncertain outcome, the outcome of which you care about, and the resulting physical and mental reaction to this worrying, which we call nervousness. Nervousness requires focusing by worrying and ruminating. There are tons of things to be worried or nervous about. Let's name some:

- I'm nervous about Parent Teacher Conferences tomorrow because I'm afraid they might say something negative about little Tommy.

- My boss has really been riding me at work. Despite my best efforts at trying harder, I cannot please her. What if I get fired?

- I only worked ten hours today and I still have clients asking me to do things. Should I take the rest of the day off and get back to them tomorrow or keep working a little more? If I quit for the day, will I feel too much anxiety to enjoy not working?

- Do I have enough money? Am I earning enough money? Am I saving enough money? Am I spending too much money?

- Money.

- My cousin is fighting cancer. What if they don't make it?

- Global warming is melting the ice caps. What if our climate is destroyed and my kids will live on an inhospitable planet?

- What if I'm not good enough tomorrow?

I could go on and on, but you get the idea, and I'm sure you have thought some of the things above. I'm sure you could also add to the list indefinitely. How do you stop worrying about these things and become at peace with yourself? The winning philosophy is espoused in Chapter 3, where we determined that *this is the same as that.* That is, to accept any circumstance with equanimity. This is the same as "God, grant me the serenity to accept the things I cannot change." While this is the silver bullet for tranquility, it is exceptionally difficult, and involves great mental tribulations and wrestling with one's own mind. So let's talk about some easier solutions.

One strategy is to stop thinking about the bulleted list above. This is also easier said than done. It only takes one worry, like a pebble in the shoe, to make us feel nervous and ruin our relaxation. One strategy I learned is to think and decide what to do about the things you can change. Again, this appears as "Courage to change the things I can." Once you have these plans, you can take these worries off your plate. If the remaining worries can't be solved, then further thinking about them is only worry, and no further thinking will result in anything productive. This is where patience comes in, with some optimism and courage, where you just say to yourself, "let's just wait and see how it goes." This thought can still perpetuate the worry, but it should quell it a bit. Finally, if some things are still worrying you, you can decide to "think about them later." Now you have a clear head and you can relax. The relaxation is attained by simultaneously increasing your physical and mental comfort and further reducing your nervousness. Here are some examples that I found particularly effective:

- Perform some deep breathing and let your mind wander and drift away from everything
  - ◊ Try to breathe deeply into your stomach
  - ◊ Close your eyes
  - ◊ Harvest positive energy when you breathe in and expel chaos and negative energy on the outbreath (this is effective if you know anything about meditation and chakras and stuff like that)
  - ◊ You can do this any time you have a spare moment. It doesn't have to be at the end of the day. I've done it on the subway, during car rides, and in the middle of the day. Cultivating such a meditation can be the break you need during a stressful day.
- Draw a bath
  - ◊ You may not have had a bath since childhood, but they are extremely relaxing
  - ◊ You can do the candle thing and the bubble thing or whatever you want or just lie in the tub
  - ◊ Read a good book while you're in the bath
  - ◊ Watch some TV
  - ◊ Online streaming content is better than ever before
  - ◊ There's entertainment for everyone
  - ◊ Watch something relatively mindless or something not very emotional. It's fun to do this before bed.
- Ride a bicycle
  - ◊ Again, you'd be surprised at how fun a bicycle is as

an adult. It's more fun to ride a bicycle as an adult in the same way as it was more fun to drive at age sixteen than it is at forty.

  - ◊ The physical activity will dissipate the nervousness

- Take a walk
  - ◊ Your mind actually performs at its best during a leisurely walk
  - ◊ Your mind will wander and you may develop solutions to things you couldn't figure out before
  - ◊ The physical activity will dissipate the nervousness
- Read a book (like you are now)
  - ◊ People don't read as much as they used to, but reading is a very relaxing, tranquil activity
- Give and receive massages with your partner
  - ◊ You don't need to go to the spa to get a great massage
  - ◊ Keep practicing on each other and eventually your partner, with the greater comfort of being touched by you, will enjoy your massages more than the ones at the spa
  - ◊ These massages often lead to internal massages
- Masturbate
  - ◊ Did you stop masturbating when you were a teenager? If so, why did you?
  - ◊ The catharsis and endorphin explosion of orgasms from masturbation are therapeutic

    - ◊ This keeps your sex organs and your circulation in practice for the real thing
    - ◊ It will relax you

- Exercise at a local gym
    - ◊ Strength training has been shown to be the most beneficial exercise if only one form of exercise is being performed
    - ◊ Higher levels of exercise trigger the recently discovered Brain Derived Neurotrophic Factor (BDNF). BDNF essentially enhances mental function and can "make you smarter."
    - ◊ Once you get into the habit of going to the gym, you will look forward to every aspect of it: going to a different place, performing the actual exercise and the exertion of it, the afterglow of the workout, and the better sleep you will get.
    - ◊ Of course, there are the long-term health and appearance benefits
    - ◊ Physically working out nerves is a real thing
- Go on a hike or immerse yourself in nature
    - ◊ Hiking, kayaking, and canoeing are all ways to immerse yourself in nature
    - ◊ The ambient sights and sounds are bound to relax you
- Get away from your cell phone, the internet, social media, and anything else where someone could get ahold of you and ruin your mood, or where content can come to your awareness and ruin your mood

- ◊ Once people know that you have off hours, they will either respect it or give up trying to get ahold of you
- ◊ If others won't respect your time, you have to be the one who does
- ◊ The feeds and chimes of media feeds will do everything they can to get your attention. After your attention is stolen, what happens to your mental state is at the whim of whatever the algorithm has chosen to display to you.

- Stretch or do some yoga
    - ◊ If you don't know how to do it, there are plenty of videos out there
    - ◊ Deep, slow stretching has a similar effect to Yoga. You can make up your own stretches if you don't want to bother learning new ones.
- Have a face-to-face
    - ◊ Talk to someone face to face. The dynamic is much faster than texting and emailing, and you don't know where the conversation will go.
    - ◊ The social experience of this dying art makes one feel more connected and relaxation can result
- Play with your dog
    - ◊ Oh, the simplicity of playing ball. It never gets old for the dog, and it will never get old for you.
- Play with your kids
    - ◊ This can sometime seem like work, but after you get

started and get into it, you will start to feel like a kid yourself

- ◊ The mindlessness of playing is beneficial to adults, and the time spent between parents and kids will be cherished for a lifetime

- Do some chores
  - ◊ Especially for people who do mental jobs, manual labor can be relaxing. Washing the truck, cleaning the bathroom, chopping firewood, and cleaning the house can actually relieve stress.
- Play some sports/games
  - ◊ Focusing on the game for a while does wonders to reduce your stress level. Just don't fret too much about winning.
- Play physical puzzles/games
  - ◊ With cell phone games and ubiquitous electronics, these are an endangered species
  - ◊ Playing with family or a group of people is an even more powerful experience now because it's so rare
- Listen to some vinyl records
  - ◊ You can listen to music in any format, but listening to vinyl tends to isolate the music listening, isolates the activity, and the sound is the best sound possible.[30]

---

30 It's almost an undisputed fact that vinyl records are the best sounding music reproduction technology, despite being the oldest. The only physical medium to increase in sales recently has been vinyl. As an interesting caveat, the mp3s or streaming audio that everyone is listening to have the same quality as an old cassette. CDs actually sound better than mp3s as well.

◊ Having to flip and change the records is inconvenient, but it serves to ensure that maybe the only thing you're doing is listening to the music. Most of the time, people are listening to music while they're doing something else. Listening to music alone is a relaxing experience.

What I have suggested above is just a sample of an endless array of activities that can reduce nervousness and increase both physical and mental comfort. The most enduring comfort comes from the deeper sense of feeling complementary or one with the universe, being completely comfortable "in your own skin," and being able to enter into meditative or transformative states by relaxation or other means. It is possible to be in a form of this state all of the time, which is called bliss, or even nirvana. Achieving this is the most difficult, but most important goal of self discovery, and it is hoped that this book is part of a path to help you get there.

CHAPTER 15: BUYING THE HOMESTEAD

Have you ever heard the saying "bought the farm?" "Buying the farm" is old Air Force slang for dying during battle. The reason it was called "buying the farm" is because when a pilot crashed into someone's farm during a battle, the farmer was entitled to insurance money from the Air Force to compensate him for the damage. A battle is normally with another entity. This entity is called the enemy. "Buying the homestead" is terminology defined here that refers to purposely crashing into one's own farm, or homestead, and having the estate, next of kin, or insurance beneficiaries pay for the damage. Buying the Homestead is my euphemism for suicide.

Suicide is not a means of escape, but, rather, the end of a battle with oneself. To think of it any other way is cruel and insensitive. One who battles the desire to kill themself and ends the battle by taking their own life is not a loser, nor are they any less than anyone who resisted the urge or never thought of it to begin with. There are scores of people who have thought about killing themselves, and maybe should have, but were too cowardly to do it.

People who commit suicide are labeled as cowards. This is not the case. Suicide takes a tremendous amount of courage. The following quote is from the movie *Cloud Atlas*, and describes the point here:

> **Robert Frobisher:** My dearest Sixsmith, I shot myself through the roof of my mouth this morning with Vivian Ayrs' Luger. A true suicide is a paced, disciplined certainty. People pontificate suicide is a coward's act. Couldn't be further from the truth. Suicide takes tremendous courage. Don't let them say I killed myself for love. Had my infatuations, but we both know in our hearts who is the sole love of my short, bright life.

Suicide is most likely to be committed by someone suffering from a mental illness. In this capacity, the person was already being subjected to the tremendously negative stigma that surrounds people with such conditions. At the time of their death, and afterwards, they will be most likely labeled as weak, selfish, and cowardly. Close ones left behind from the suicide will have to endure these labels. Indeed, the survivors of suicide refrain from even telling anyone that they had family members who took their own lives. With friends, it's a little different, and people tend to be less sensitive to sharing the information that their friend decided to take their own life.

My father took his own life when I was twenty years old. He was just forty years old. He still had half his life ahead of him. The spookiest thing for me is that I will soon be older than he was when he died. No one should become the elder of their parents, even if it's just the memory of their elders. There isn't a more painful way for a loved one to die. Not only are they out of your life forever, but you are also left with the feeling that your relationship with them and your love for them were not enough to sustain their desire to live. But, like I said, suicide is the result of a battle with oneself. It may be prompted, in its finality, by a divorce, a break up, or the death of another loved one, but ultimately it's a self-battle. An expression of suicide can look something like this:

$$P(\textit{suicide}):\ (\textit{Present Pain} + \textit{Projected Future Pain}) > (\textit{Potential Future Life Enjoyment}) \times (\textit{Chance of a Better Future Life})$$

Where : P(suicide) = the probability of committing suicide

Present Pain = the level of current pain: physical, emotional, mental, and spiritual

Projected Future Pain = this is the belief of how much pain one will face or endure in the future. It is normally related to the Present Pain, and is often unrealistic in its projections because of this.

Potential Future Life Enjoyment = this is basically the opposite of "projected future pain," and is related to how hopeful one is about the future. People committing suicide often have no hope for the future, and don't believe that anything in their future lives could make them happy. On the other hand, if there is a single event, or sliver of hope that makes this term impossibly large, it could be enough to prevent suicide. This could be meeting the love of one's life, having children, or becoming famous.

Chance of a Better Future Life = this is the assigned probability in one's mind that one's life will get better. If one sees nothing changing for the positive, this value will be very low. If one sees positive events, is confident for change, and is optimistic for other positive things in the future, this value will be higher.

So, the chances of someone committing suicide are higher if their present pain and belief in how much future pain they will have is higher. It is lower if they believe their chances of a better life are higher and if that future life is projected to be enjoyable. To make things simpler: a pessimistic worldview increases the chances of suicide, and an optimistic worldview decreases the chances of suicide.

There are other variables and conditions for suicide. For some people, often parents, there are slivers of life left or things that must be accomplished in the future before one finally chooses take one's own life. These leftover things could be things like raising some or all of your children until "they don't need you anymore[31] your finances are arranged such that your dependents will be taken care of upon your death, or, perhaps the most tragically, someone else has been murdered or an appropriate form of revenge has taken place. The suicide expression becomes expanded as:

$$\textit{P(suicide): (Present Pain + Projected Future Pain)} > \textit{(Potential Future Life Enjoyment) x (Chance of a Better Future Life)} \xrightarrow{\text{and when}} \textit{(Special Condition is Satisfied)}$$

Even this equation is too simple, because the fear of death is a huge factor that often prevents or permits suicide. The fear of death is the fear of the unknown. The largest unknown is,

31 Actually, they will always need you.

perhaps, death.[32] We can't imagine not being, for not being requires us to not be able to imagine. We can't imagine not being able to imagine. Of course, this view of death is simply the belief that, after death, we simply cease to be. There are many other beliefs about what actually happens after you die. There are visions of heaven, fears of hell, reincarnation, becoming one with the universe, and a multitude of other things. There are also others who say, "I don't know," but they still have to resist the urge to think about it.

Sadly, the belief that one is instantly transported into a sort of heaven after one takes one's own life is a driver for suicide. I know this for a fact, because both my father and my cousin stated this as prime reasons for taking their own lives. My father was a very religious man, although he practiced in relative solitude. He was of the Christian faith. Some doctrines of Christianity teach that people who commit suicide go to hell. I know my father heard this and believed it for some time. Indeed, it probably kept him alive for many years. However, he eventually came to the conclusion, with the counsel of a pastor, that he would still go to heaven if he killed himself, especially since he had a mental illness. Surely the almighty God would take that into account and grant an exception, if hell for suicides was a general rule. So my dad condemned this life, and reserved his happiness for the heaven that would surely come after it. In his suicide note and last words, he expressed hope for happiness in heaven.

Had my dad been an atheist, or still believed that suicides result in a one-way ticket to hell, he may not have killed himself. This is a grand irony of suicide that cannot be overstated: glamorous visions of the afterlife or things to come after death greatly

---

32 Notwithstanding the fact that, earlier, we stated that death is the same as how it was before you were born.

increase the chances of someone killing themselves. The fear of the unknown is sufficient to prevent a lot of suicides. When this unknown becomes "known" via beliefs, there is a high chance for trouble. So, adding this to our probability of suicide expression, we have:

$$P(\text{suicide}): \frac{(\text{Present Pain} + \text{Projected Future Pain})}{(\text{Fear of Death})} > \frac{(\text{Potential Future Life Enjoyment}) \times (\text{Chance of a Better Future Life})}{(\text{Fear of Death})} \xrightarrow{\text{and when}} (\text{Special Condition is Satisfied})$$

The (Fear of Death) factor accounts for the person's belief in what happens in the afterlife and how good or bad that afterlife will be. Conversely, the fear of death accounts for a belief that death precedes total nonexistence. Suicide is contagious. A person who is related to someone who has killed themselves is more likely to take their own life than a person who is in an otherwise normal family. This was true in my own family. My cousin took his own life two years after my father did. Leading up to his suicide, he was quoted saying things like, "My uncle had it right. There is nothing in this life for me. I need to get out like he did." My cousin's last words, moments before he hung himself during a party at his house, were, "I am going to see my uncle now." The people at this party didn't know that his uncle had killed himself.

So, this trail of suicides leads me to ask the obvious question: would my cousin have killed himself if my dad hadn't first? I don't know, but knowing that someone else has killed themselves is like knowing someone who was courageous enough to ride a scary roller coaster, and who chose that roller coaster to ride on. It makes you more likely to do it. Knowing somebody, anybody, who has killed themselves is also like listening to a negative commentary on life and potentially soliciting a belief in the afterlife. Both my father and cousin were sure of the fact that they were going to heaven.

If you consider that the afterlife spans eternity, or eons at least, then the eighty years we spend here are nothing compared to the afterlife. Our lives are a mere footnote in the existence of an eternal being. A lot of people speak of an eternal life, or eternal life after this life. It makes no sense. The definition of eternity is "lasting or existing forever; without end or beginning." The very fact that our lives here have a beginning, or that our lives in heaven would have an inception, means that neither one of those lives, or those lives together, could be eternal. Even if you could live for thousands and thousands of years, eventually you would begin to forget, and continue to forget, your earlier years, and each time this happens would be like a new life beginning.

Eternal life is impossible. In order for there to be life, there has to be death. One could say that death's very existence is the only thing that gives life life. Without death, life would have no purpose at all. That's not true? Think of what you would do if you had an infinite amount of time to do it, you had no need to clothe yourself, you had no need to eat, there was no need for sex, and you figured why start doing something now, when you have all the time in the world? Let's examine the seven characteristics of living things that we all learned in fifth grade Life Sciences:

1. Nutrition Living things take in materials from their surroundings that they use for growth or to provide energy. Nutrition is the process by which organisms

obtain energy and raw materials from nutrients such as proteins, carbohydrates and fats.

2. Respiration Respiration is the release of energy from food substances in all living cells. Living things break down food within their cells to release energy for carrying out the following processes.
3. Movement All living things move. It is very obvious that a leopard moves but what about the thorn tree it sits in? Plants too move in various different ways. The movement may be so slow that it is very difficult to see.
4. Excretion All living things excrete. As a result of the many chemical reactions occurring in cells, they have to get rid of waste products which might poison the cells. Excretion is defined as the removal of toxic materials, the waste products of metabolism and substances in excess from the body of an organism.
5. Growth Growth is seen in all living things. It involves using food to produce new cells. The permanent increase in cell number and size is called growth.
6. Reproduction All living organisms have the ability to produce offspring.
7. Sensitivity All living things are able to sense and respond to stimuli around them such as light, temperature, water, gravity and chemical substances.

While these seven things are characteristics of living things, it can easily be stated that these are all characteristics of things that can die, that are trying to prevent death, or that need to propagate the species because of death. What's more, a being with eternal life would cease to do those things, or would not have to do those things, and would not be a living thing as we know it.

Suicide is said to be a selfish act, but the people who survive the person who lost their life in their battle for self sometimes act very selfishly. Here are some selfish examples of things that survivors say in response to suicide:

1. He took the easy way out. He should have stuck it out with the rest of us.
2. He left us all to fend for ourselves. Why didn't he think of that before he killed himself?
3. He must not have loved me that much at all if he left me here like this all alone.
4. I don't want to end up killing myself like my father did.
5. Only crazy people kill themselves. I'll never do that.
6. He left as much of a mess of his estate and beneficiaries as he had in his life before he died.
7. I knew he was going to do that at some point or another.
8. He had the right idea. I might end up doing that someday. Life sucks.

Now, here are compassionate ways of expressing the antonym of each of these statements:

1. Things must have been really rough for him in order for him to do that. I wish I had known he felt that way so I could've gotten him some help.
2. Fending for himself was more impossible to think of than helping others fend for themselves. His overwhelming

battle for himself probably did think of you, but, in the end, it was his battle for himself that killed him.

3. He might have loved you so much that he wanted to spare you from any future harm he thought he might have caused you. Or, he was confident that you would be able to make it yourself.
4. I will live my life and not repeat my father's mistakes. I hope that if I live my life this way, I will not have the urge to kill myself.
5. Crazy people kill themselves and so do normal people. Being crazy is not the only factor in suicide, although certain mental conditions increase the chances that one will succumb to it.
6. If I would have helped him clean up his mess of a life, maybe he wouldn't have left it.
7. I knew he was in trouble, so I tried helping him.
8. If I live a similar pattern of behavior as he did, I may want to kill myself. If I live a good life and surround myself with good things, I probably won't want to kill myself. If I do feel like killing myself, I will seek help to prevent it, or use other techniques to convince myself that it's not worth it.

The suicide survivor tends to think of themselves. This will always cause bitterness and enmity towards the one who killed themselves. The person who killed themselves should get the same reverence and honor that a soldier fallen in battle gets, that a military veteran gets, and that someone who has succumbed to a chronic disease like cancer gets. A person who committed suicide gets scorned, labeled as the ultimate loser, labeled as the ultimate coward, and his life gets brought up less because others want to avoid thinking about how he died.

I had a lot of anger towards my father after he killed himself. I had so much anger that I wasn't really that sad that he died. After all, my father frequently told me he loved me and that I was a special fixture of his life. When he killed himself, all that love that I had heard about over all of those years was erased. After all, if he loved me as much as he said, he wouldn't kill himself and be away from me, right? I resorted to remembering everything negative my father had ever done in my life. I ignored the positive things. I tried to foster a feeling of hatred for him. "I don't want to end up being a loser and killing myself like my father did," I would say. When I met people, they would ask about my parents. Every single time they asked about my dad it was a stab in the heart, and it increased my anger that I had to deal with embarrassment because of him. I had to feel embarrassed by him after his death, in addition to all of the crazy drunk things he did while he was alive. These feelings were like a black stain, or ooze, that covered my true feelings for my father. How could I love someone who betrayed the love that they had confessed for me?

The release from my woes stemming from my father's suicide came in the form of being diagnosed with the same illness he had. This was the illness that killed him. Bipolar disorder. I tried managing it through the years, and I eventually started doing a good job. In the middle of that, I was going through a terrible bout of depression. My soul hurt and seared at the same time, my mind was on fire with torment, but I had a lack of energy or desire to continue with life. I thought of all of the terrible things I had to endure in my life. Why? *Why did I have to go through those things?* I screamed in my mind. I started sobbing for myself and everything that I had gone through. A very strong urge to take my own life started rising to the surface. I was really considering it. I was shocked. I was horrified. The feelings weren't born from an ordinary brain. I knew that they were from my illness. At this instant, I knew exactly how and why my father had taken his own life. A wash of forgiveness came down that scoured my blackened heart for him. I forgave him. I wept. I never knew such pain could bring about so much forgiveness and love. I wondered if the entire point of me having his illness was so that I could forgive him and understand what he went through.

However, my forgiveness for my father did make me realize some things. It made me realize that his failure to manage his illness is what led to him not being able to resist the urge to kill himself. It made me realize that the sins of his life also contributed to his suicide. I vowed to manage my illness and live a good life, for the actual sake of my life, and not just for a good life. Learning from his mistakes is what helped me become the man I've become. I'm thankful for the sins and mistakes of my father. His memorial, as a fallen soldier, is my life, and the memory of my life that I will pass on to those after me.

To memorialize the fallen, my son's first name is that of my cousin who died, and his middle name is my father's. I don't want to forget or hide what they did. I don't want to be proud of what they did, but I want to honor and respect it. Suicide is not a coward's way out. It's a tragic loss in the ultimate battle of self. People should stop being self centered and judgmental when they think or hear of people who have killed themselves. No one should be embarrassed that their father, mother, brother, son, cousin, friend, or anyone they knew, killed themselves. This embarrassment kills them more each day.

CHAPTER 16: EMOTIONAL MECHANICS: STOPPING PI(E)

Emotional Mechanics, which is the title of this book, is the title of this chapter. This chapter echoes the definitions, relationships, equations, understanding and concepts developed hitherto and how to conflate them to temper emotions, ignite passions, change your mind, keep a consistent mindset, stay on target, or shift to another target. This chapter also discusses sources of motivation to change your life, the ultimate fears we all face, and a way to reconcile these fears and feel unity with all life and the universe as a whole.

We all possess a rational mind that can balance concepts and make choices on the basis of numbers, facts, money, and other concrete concepts. However, we all know that decisions aren't made on the basis of these concrete concepts; they are made based on emotions. In fact, there are people with certain types of brain damage which prohibits them from feeling emotions[33] , and they are unable to make even simple decisions like what milk to buy at the grocery store. This inability to make decisions stems from a lack of the ability to assign relative weights to different decisions using emotions. Clearly, it is our emotions that drive our choices, and it is our choices that drive our lives. In order to get a handle on your life, you must first get a handle on your emotions.

Emotional mechanics has to start with motivation. Motivation is preceded by a desire to change. A desire to change is prompted by an observation that something isn't okay. So, the first step in emotional mechanics is to notice something negative about your life. The issue with this is that the observation can be too big or too small to be actionable. Here are some examples of observations that may not be suitable to effect change:

1. I only express my emotions when I'm drunk.
   - ◊ This is a good realization, but if one keeps on receiving catharsis from emotional drunken stupors, this won't prompt any change.
2. All I can think of is work and work related things.
   - ◊ This is an incomplete observation or realization. This person would also have to realize that having only work in his life is not enough. He should also want family, recreation, and personal hobbies to be in his life react to this observation.
3. I'm lonely.
   - ◊ Are you alone and lonely, or lonely even when you're with people? Was there a recent time when

33 Please see the article at https://www.thecut.com/2016/06/how-only-using-logic-destroyed-a-man.html for examples of people with this ailment

you weren't lonely? Did you push people away from you and your life?

4. I can't relax.
   - ◊ Why can't you relax? How do you try to relax and how do you fail?
   - ◊ What do you worry about while you're trying to relax?

These four observations alone are insufficient to effect change because their origins are unknown. It is like trying to cure a disease by merely suppressing its symptoms or trying to put out a fire by eliminating its smoke. The root of the behavior needs to be found in order to change or eliminate it. Using the same four examples above, here are some realizations and insights that might empower one to eliminate these problems:

1. I only express my emotions when I'm drunk.
   - ◊ When I'm sober, I am reluctant to share my emotions because I am afraid of appearing weak and I am terrified of what others may think of me after I express my emotions.
   - ◊ I can slowly build up the courage to share my emotions when I'm sober, starting with more superficial ones, and see if I feel the same release as I do when I'm drunk doing the same thing.
   - ◊ It may become unnecessary to get drunk to share my feelings and I may drink less as a result of this.
2. All I can think of is work and work related things.
   - ◊ I value financial security more than anything else in life. This isn't because I'm a miser, it's because

I'm afraid of what might happen to me and my family if a financial catastrophe were to occur. I am insulating myself from the fear by earning as much money as I can.

◊ I can realize that losing my job, having a natural disaster destroy my things, or the economy crashing can cause financial catastrophe. This risk of financial loss may be greater than the risk of me not working hard enough, so I should not worry about finances as much and realize that I am not in total control of my financial destiny anyway. Accepting this, I can focus less on work and more on other things in my life.

3. I'm lonely.

◊ It may not be that I feel lonely, but I experience a lack of belonging. I need to find a sense of belonging in my family, my work, and possibly by engaging in hobbies with a group or individual. I gravitate towards others in order to feel this belonging, and I don't feel loneliness anymore.

4. I can't relax.

◊ The fast pace of life, the demands of work and family, and the persistent feeling that I have to keep up with technology have me constantly worried.

◊ I can't change the stressful aspects of society, but I can control how I react to it. I know that most of my worrying does nothing productive, but I am scared of not worrying. I am scared of missing something that may harm me. I decide to relegate my worrying time to specific times during the day. I make this into a habit. During my designated worry times, I address all of my concerns and feel protected that I addressed specific vulnerabilities.

◊ I realize that worrying isn't in itself bad, but being consumed by it is.

Identifying and eliminating the source is sometimes all that is necessary to solve life problems. However, the inspection of some problems may reveal that there are actually multiple layers, or root branches, that are necessary to uncover or uproot to eliminate the ultimate source. This is a painful and grueling practice, because the light at the end of the tunnel is covered. Often, digging out one root may produce more roots, or more problems, than were there to begin with. There is a saying that attempts to state the source of all roots, or evil.

THE LOVE OF MONEY IS THE ROOT OF ALL EVIL

First, let's present the source and, more importantly, the context of this statement "The Love of Money is the Root of All Evil"[34] This statement originates in the sixth chapter of the Book of Timothy in the New Testament, and verses four, six, seven, eight, nine, ten, seventeen, and eighteen are repeated here:

4 He is proud, knowing nothing, but doting about questions and strifes of words, whereof cometh envy, strife, railings, evil surmisings,

6 But godliness with contentment is great gain.

34 This quote is most often incorrectly quoted as "Money is the root of all evil."

7 For we brought nothing into this world, and it is certain we can carry nothing out.

8 And having food and raiment let us be therewith content.

9 But they that will be rich fall into temptation and a snare, and into many foolish and hurtful lusts, which drown men in destruction and perdition.

10 For the love of money is the root of all evil: which while some coveted after, they have erred from the faith, and pierced themselves through with many sorrows.

17 Charge them that are rich in this world, that they be not highminded, nor trust in uncertain riches, but in the living God, who giveth us richly all things to enjoy;

18 That they do good, that they be rich in good works, ready to distribute, willing to communicate;

Verse four states that the ignorant man chooses to argue, and that such arguing is the cause of evil. This is the man who values being right above all things, and fights as if to the death over arguments, debates, and matters of fact. His money, his system of value is ruling arguments and he becomes more prideful in doing so. Verse four states that a person with this mindset is ignorant.

Verse six states, paradoxically, that great gain is being content[35] and not pursuing anything for gain. Verse seven is basically the First Law of Thermodynamics, that energy can neither be created nor destroyed—just transformed—such that there is no measure to the fruits or weeds of one's life.

---

35 In Chapter 14, the referenced song declared "contentment expresses tenderness."

Verse nine states that the desire for hurtful and foolish things causes sorrow. This echoes the Buddha, who stated that desire is the cause of suffering.

Verse ten is almost always confused. It is referring to money, but not in the literal sense of how we think about money. It's referring to the symbol of money and what it represents. Money represents a systematic method of assigning value, gain, and loss to items, services, and commodities. In this biblical sense, money represents assigning value to being right, having power, experiencing positive emotions, and anything else, tangible or intangible, that is considered positive and worth seeking. It was already stated that nothing can be gained or lost during one's lifetime, so assigning a value to anything is actually the root of all evil. For there are no things that are more important than other things, or people who are more important than others, because there is an infinite number of number of perspectives and ways of weighting things and people, and, fortunately, most of these perspective and ways are unknown to us It is plausible, given the infinite number of possibilities of life that all things and people are of equal importance.

Verses sixteen and seventeen are not necessarily referring to people who have lots of money, but rather people who have godly wisdom, pure hearts, favors to give without reciprocation, and good works, and that these "rich people" distribute these good works freely.

AFRAID OF LOSING YOURSELF

After a long string of bad events in my life, I came home to an empty apartment where my wife, who I was attempting to reconcile with, had decided not to reconcile and left me with nothing.

It felt like someone pierced my soul with a blazing sword. That night, while sleeping on the floor, I kept staring up at the ceiling and wondering, "Why do these bad things keep on happening to me?" I had a sick feeling in my stomach and chest. I thought this was due to her leaving me as she did, but it wasn't. I accepted that she had left and it didn't bother me so much. Something else was there.

"What am I really afraid of?" I kept asking myself again and again in my mind, and in my heart. Losing my children and my wife to divorce felt like a death of part of me, yet there I still was. I thought of my father, who died prematurely by suicide, and his death was also a death of part of me, yet there I still was. I kept on reciting all of the bad things that happened to me throughout my life. I thought of my current fears. I feared that I would become a loser, never find love, and never realize some of the dreams I had. I also feared that I would lose my health, my career, and my sanity.

Then it dawned on me, a silver lining, a sliver of sunlight through a drawn shade: *I'm afraid of losing myself.* This immediately struck a chord, and I knew it was an absolute truth. All of my past losses and fears of future loss were merely fears of losing part of myself and, ultimately, my total self. A lifetime of past losses and possible future losses coalesced into this one fear. I had unearthed the source root, but I did not know how to pull it out. *How can I not be afraid of losing myself?* Certainly, the fear of dying was part of that fear, but it was better described as the fear of losing my ego. Losing my ego might happen at death, and it can certainly happen during life. I realized I had been losing myself my entire life: changing, growing, meeting new people, saying goodbye to people, and succumbing to the constant change that life is. I had lost myself a million times, through both good and bad things. This still was not enough to comfort me.

I considered how the totality of who I was at that time was based on the entire universe around me, and not just me as an isolated thing. I also knew that part of me, in some way, would endure after my physical death, even if it was just my atoms becoming a tree or something like that. After all, we're all just made of stardust.

The universe, and any god with it, was intertwined with me. I couldn't escape it, and it couldn't escape me. I was it and it was me. *There was no me!* Christ said in Matthew 16:24-25:

> 24 Then said Jesus unto his disciples, If any man will come after me, let him deny himself, and take up his cross, and follow me.
>
> 25 For whosoever will save his life shall lose it: and whosoever will lose his life for my sake shall find it.

I denied "my" life. There was no "my life." There was simply life, and I was an integral part of it. I lost my life, and, in doing so, found it. This was the happiest moment of my life, and hot, joyful tears streamed down my face. I wept with joy for what seemed like an eternity. I could still pursue things, enjoy things, but not like my life depended on it. Because it didn't. The universe depended on me, and I the universe. The Father is the Son, and the Son is the Father. This is the true Revelation as depicted in the New Testament.

STOPPING PI(E)

Stopping pie is ceasing the pursuit of desires to fulfill one's life. It is like a dog chasing its own tail. With one weed pulled out, several more will grow in its place. The pursuit of earthly riches is endless. Pie is the dessert of life that we all wait for or try to eat. Eating pie is eating the notion of the forbidden fruit, which is thinking one thing has more value than another.

STOPPING PI

Stopping Pi is the ceasing of something spinning around a circle for an eternity. Stopping Pi is arresting the progression of infinite, unknown numbers that represents an unstoppable cycle of pain. In our final equation, we can summarize stopping pi:[36]

$$\pi = C/D$$

$$\pi D = C$$

Where:

π=unknown circular path

C=Your encapsulated life with an unknown value

D=you, or how you measure you

A life of C, encapsulated with an unknown value, represents a life measured arbitrarily and in isolation. That is, C is ended

36 The distance around a circle can be found by multiplying the number Pi, which can be approximated as 3.14 but actually has an infinite sequence of numbers after 3.14..., by the circle's diameter, which is a known value. The value of the circumference is always an approximation because Pi is an unknown, infinite number.

when death happens, and its value is unknown. This results in an unsatisfying life and death. Thus, we need to redefine D:

Either:

D=0,there is no me

therefore:

$\pi = C/0$

$\pi = \infty$

Which means:

$\infty 0 = C$

C=indeterminate

C=is not encapsulated and cannot be defined and most likely goes on forever

There is also an alternate approach to stopping pi. Most things in nature and the proportion of things that grow naturally follow the Fibonacci Sequence, which can be used to define the golden ratio. The golden ratio is:

$$\frac{(a+b)}{a} = \frac{a}{b} = \varphi = \frac{1+\sqrt{5}}{2} = 1.6180339887\ldots$$

The Fibonacci Sequence is the sequence of numbers that starts with 0 followed by any value, and then each successive number is the sum of the previous two numbers. If the first number after 0 is 1, then the Fibonacci Sequence is: 0, 1, 1, 2, 3, 5, 8, 13, 21, 34, 55, 89... When you divide a number by its previous number in the sequence, the ratio begins to approach the golden ratio. If the numbers are expanded to infinity, the ratio is the golden ratio. As an example, 89/55=1.61818... The beauty of the Fibonacci Sequence is that its next number depends on the number before it, and the entire series is based on whatever was chosen to be the first number. The first number can be any number. That value can be completely random, and that random number may be the variation in each life that is born. This sequence represents how trees grow, mountains are formed, and indeed, even the ratios of different human body parts.

Stopping pi again with the golden ratio:

$D=\varphi$, I grow naturally from myself as the universe

$$C=\pi\varphi$$

Which expands to:

$$C=\pi(0+1+2+3+5+8+13...)$$

C, your life, can now be seen to be an ever expanding spiral whose form is somewhat known and that expands based on its previous history. C, the universe, can now be seen to be an ever expanding spiral whose form is somewhat known and that expands based on its previous history. Somehow the universe, and you, started at zero, although zero can be used to produce infinity. In graphic form, it is expressed as:[37]

37 The infinity ribbon binding the "legs" of Pi represent complete ego contraction and expansion to arrive at this conclusion.

And this symbol represents using a bounded paradox to encapsulate not only your life, which is intertwined with the universe, but also the universe as a whole. Indeed, the symbol represents Stopping Pi, Stopping Pie, arresting the endless cycle of pursuing vanity, and a sanctuary of peace from the fears of death and losing yourself.

ABOUT THE AUTHOR

Yochanan Stoppi grew up with a father who had a mental illness, which eventually led to his suicide. Later in life, Yochanan developed a mental illness himself, and this dual experience of having a mental illness and watching someone with one gave him a broader perspective of mental illness. Yochanan, at certain points in his life, developed and overcame alcohol misuse, sexual promiscuity, divorce, financial troubles, smoking cigarettes, obesity, musculoskeletal disorders, and poor health in general. He leads a local support group at a community center near his home.

Yochanan is an engineer by education and training. He has used this scientific and engineering training in developing the approach, reasoning, and relationships presented herein. He is also self-taught in many subjects, including, but not limited to: philosophy, medicine, alternative medicine, health, nutrition, cosmology, physics, Taoism, meditation, counseling, and leading support groups. His favorite philosopher is Alan Watts, and he enjoys an eclectic array of music genres.

Yochanan resides with his wife, kids, and boston terrier. When not spending time with his family or working, he enjoys bicycling, hiking, and learning. He is a Master Mason in Freemasonry.